The Perils of Social Media

The Perils of Social Media

Cyberbullying Shame and Fame

Merve Basdogan

ROWMAN & LITTLEFIELD
Lanham • Boulder • New York • London

Rowman & Littlefield
Bloomsbury Publishing Inc, 1385 Broadway, New York, NY 10018, USA
Bloomsbury Publishing Plc, 50 Bedford Square, London, WC1B 3DP, UK
Bloomsbury Publishing Ireland, 29 Earlsfort Terrace, Dublin 2, D02 AY28, Ireland
www.rowman.com

British Library Cataloguing in Publication Information Available

Library of Congress Cataloging-in-Publication Data Available

ISBN 978-1-4758-5421-3 (cloth : alk. paper)
ISBN 978-1-4758-5422-0 (pbk. : alk. paper)
ISBN 978-1-4758-5423-7 (ebook)

For product safety related questions contact productsafety@bloomsbury.com.

∞™ The paper used in this publication meets the minimum requirements of American
National Standard for Information Sciences—Permanence of Paper for Printed Library
Materials, ANSI/NISO Z39.48-1992.

Contents

Preface

When I was a graduate student at Indiana University School of Education, I took a course called "Biology of Behavior." It was in this class that I first began to explore the reasons behind our actions, the changes in our brain and psychology, and the theories that explain these transformations. Questions like why some people are more aggressive than others and why some tend to be victims intrigued me deeply.

As a curious graduate student, I found the social experiments and discussions in that class very captivating. For instance, we studied classic experiments like the Bobo Doll experiment, where children observed adults acting aggressively toward a toy clown and then imitated the behavior themselves. Another memorable experiment was the Marshmallow Test, which tested children's self-control by offering them a choice between one marshmallow now or two if they waited. These discussions and readings provided profound insights into human behavior, especially in how environmental factors, family, norms, culture, medium, learning space, and peers shape our actions.

I was especially inspired by that course's instructor, Dr. David Estell, an associate professor of human development. His passion for the subject was infectious, and his untimely passing later left me deeply sad.

As a scholar of educational technology, I began to connect what I learned in this course to technology. I was curious about how our interactions change when mediated through technology and how different online spaces influence behavior. This book was born out of a final assignment where I reviewed literature on the changing discourse of cyberbullying intervention and prevention strategies. That paper evolved into a conference presentation at the 2019 American Educational Research Association (AERA) annual meeting in Toronto.

At the conference, a chance encounter changed the direction of my work. Carlie Wall from Rowman and Littlefield attended my presentation and, with a genuine smile, expressed interest in my research after my session. She asked if I would consider turning my paper into a book, and without hesitation, I said yes. "Writing a book," it was a dream come true—one I had cherished since high school when I fell in love with the vivid storytelling in novels like *A Thousand Splendid Suns* by Khaled Hosseini, *Evening Class* by Maeve Binchy, and *The Clown and His Daughter* by Halide Edip Adıvar. These authors transported me to different worlds, making me feel the sunshine in Mariam's hair, the humor and warmth of an Italian evening class, and the dilemmas faced by Rabia in that poor Ottoman-era Istanbul neighborhood.

Those authors portrayed complex emotions and societal issues such as love, jealousy, power, politics, leadership, religion, and oppression through their literary works. Though I am not writing a novel, I aim to synthesize human behaviors in a similar way in this book, but in the context of cyberbullying and through a scientific lens informed by research.

Although I do not have a strong assertion that you will remember this book as vividly as I remember my cherished high school reads, I hope it provides insights that can be applied at some point in your life. It explores themes of online self-presentation, cyberdating abuse, online gaming, the psychology of trolling, harmful social media trends, and strategies for cyberbullying intervention and prevention.

When I received the book contract offer, I was thrilled and ran to my advisor, Dr. Curtis Bonk. We met at a coffeehouse in Bloomington, Indiana, and together we went over the book contract. His advice on negotiating terms, coming from someone who has written more than a dozen books, is a cherished memory that still makes me smile.

I am now writing this preface from Lubbock, Texas. Although I eagerly accepted the offer in 2 seconds, it took over four years to complete this book. During this time, we faced the historic and tragic COVID-19 pandemic, experienced job and institutional changes, adapted to new libraries, lives, and perspectives, yet here I am, finally completing it.

I would like to express my deepest gratitude to Zulfukar Ozdogan for his unwavering support. He had a knack for catching me in the middle of my best procrastination moments with his cheerful reminders: "It's a bright and shiny day to write a book!"

To my family in Turkey, who endured years of separation, I miss you and thank you for your long-distance support. In particular, my mom, Mahi Basdogan, has been asking about my book with great excitement, eagerly waiting for the moment she will receive her signed copy. Your patience and encouragement have meant the world to me.

This book is the culmination of years of learning and exploration. I hope it serves as a valuable resource and a testament to the interconnectedness of human behavior and technology.

With heartfelt thanks,
Merve Basdogan

Introduction

It was the middle of the night when John's phone rang. On the other end was his grandson, sounding distressed. He said he was stranded at the airport, his credit cards weren't working, and he needed help. He asked John to send $2,000 so he could buy a new ticket. Without hesitation, John sent the money. His grandson thanked him, and John went back to sleep. However, when John called him the next morning, his grandson sounded confused. "What are you talking about, Grandpa? I'm sleeping in my dorm room."

This story exemplifies the common scamming tactics used to deceive people and steal their money and identity. Such schemes often target the most vulnerable, particularly individuals aged sixty-five and above, who are at the core of the digital exclusion phenomenon (Seifert et al., 2023). Additionally, children are also highly susceptible to digital scams. Teaching basic computer literacy, information literacy, media literacy, and online communication skills is essential. With the advancement of artificial intelligence (AI), these skills are becoming increasingly important as AI technologies can easily replicate voices, images, writing styles, and signatures, making it easier than ever to fall victim to cybercrimes and cyberaggression.

In this book, I define cyberbullying as any behavior conducted through electronic or digital media by individuals or groups that persistently delivers hostile or aggressive messages aimed at causing harm or discomfort to others. The target audience of this book includes anyone interested in understanding the prevalence of certain cyberbullying behaviors and the potential theories behind them to better understand their nature. This book is also designed to be used as a textbook for cyberbullying training or workshops. Instructors can easily turn each chapter into training modules and create asynchronous courses. The content and language can be adjusted to suit different age groups. Each chapter includes learning objectives at the beginning and concludes with

"Reflect and Reframe" questions that can be used as discussion prompts in a class. I have provided versions of these questions for both adults and children.

I organized the book to explore how teenagers present themselves online, the challenges they encounter, and the strategies that can help them engage with the digital world safely and healthily.

CHAPTER 1: TEENS AND SELF-PRESENTATION ON SOCIAL MEDIA

This chapter investigates how teens curate their online personas and the psychological impacts of striving for digital perfection. We explore theories of self-presentation and self-disclosure and discuss negative outcomes such as digital self-harm.

CHAPTER 2: CYBERDATING ABUSE AMONG TEENS

Here, we reviewed the literature on cyberdating abuse, examining the dynamics of trust and attachment in digital relationships. I also outlined various forms of cyberdating abuse and their implications.

CHAPTER 3: ONLINE GAMES AND CYBERBULLYING

This chapter covers the intersection of online gaming and cyberbullying, providing safety tips for parents and discussing ethical dilemmas. It also explores how promoting positive interactions in online games can be achieved through Social Exchange Theory.

CHAPTER 4: THE PSYCHOLOGY OF ONLINE TROLLING

I investigate the motivations and personality traits behind online trolling, including disruptive behaviors like photobombing and Zoombombing. The chapter also offers strategies for dealing with trolls.

CHAPTER 5: HARMFUL SOCIAL MEDIA TRENDS

This chapter examines various harmful social media trends, such as "bed rotting," and dangerous online challenges. In addition, I conducted a qualitative analysis of online comments on Reddit and YouTube to better understand what society thinks about these issues.

CHAPTER 6: PREVENTION AND INTERVENTION STRATEGIES

The final chapter provides actionable strategies to prevent and address cyber-bullying. Topics include open communication, digital hygiene, and empathy training, along with practical activities and curriculum design examples to foster a supportive digital community.

I hope you find these chapters enjoyable and full of useful tips. Together, we can work toward creating safer online spaces and supporting everyone in tackling the challenges they encounter.

Chapter 1

Teens and Self-Presentation on Social Media

LEARNING OBJECTIVES

Upon completion of this chapter, you will be able to:

1. Describe the concepts of frontstage and backstage self-presentation and how they apply to teenagers' use of social media.
2. Identify the psychological and social implications of self-presentation strategies among teenagers on social media platforms.
3. Analyze the phenomenon of digital self-harm and its underlying motivations and consequences.
4. Evaluate the role of peer influences and cultural contexts in shaping teenagers' self-presentation and self-disclosure behaviors on social media.

THE TRUMAN SHOW

In the 1998 film *The Truman Show*, Jim Carrey stars as Truman Burbank, a man whose every move is broadcast to a global audience, all without his knowledge. Midway through the film, Truman gradually realizes that his entire life has been a meticulously crafted illusion designed for the entertainment of others. Each morning, as I sip my coffee and scroll through my social media accounts, I think about *The Truman Show*. Carefully curated images, words, stories, and moments.

Self-presentation is crucial for managing impressions and projecting an online identity (Walther, 1996). The evolution of technology has provided increasingly sophisticated ways to represent ourselves online. This progression has moved from simple textual descriptions to graphical avatars in anonymous and pseud-onymous chat rooms and message boards and now to profile photos and selfies on non-anonymous social media platforms (Kapidzic & Herring, 2014).

In an era dominated by online environments and digital tools, teenagers, commonly defined as individuals aged thirteen to nineteen, have unprec-edented opportunities to learn, grow, and connect with their peers. For example, social media platforms have become integral to their lives, offering a space for self-expression, creativity, and social interaction. A recent study surveyed 1,316 U.S. teens in 2022 and findings showed that 97 percent of teens say they use the internet daily (PEW Research Center, 2022), with You-Tube, TikTok, Instagram, and Snapchat being the most popular social media platforms. In addition, 46 percent of teens say they use the internet almost constantly, according to the same survey.

This hyperconnectivity facilitated by technology is continually bringing us closer together in the online sphere. However, this growing interconnect-edness causes a strong correlation between cyberbullying and detrimental effects on mental health and psychosocial well-being (Kwan et al., 2020).

In this book, I define cyberbullying as "any behavior performed through electronic or digital media by individuals or groups that repeatedly commu-nicates hostile or aggressive messages intended to inflict harm or discomfort on others" (Tokunaga, 2010, p. 278).

This chapter is concerned with the interaction between cyberbullying and teenagers' self-presentation practices. We are going to examine digital shame, the overall psychological negative outcomes of self-presentation strat-egies, and digital self-harm.

CURATING THE PERFECT SELF: DIGITAL SHAME

Identity development is a lifelong process, and it is intense in teens (Marcia, 1980). This dynamic process is influenced greatly by peers (Davis, 2012), and teens experiment with various self-presentations to fit social norms (Giletta et al., 2021). Increasing digital interactions provide new avenues for self-expression and identity exploration. AI-supported face-enhancing filters, editing tools, and other features are used to modify their appearance and pres-ent an idealized version of themselves.

Erving Goffman, a renowned sociologist, introduced the concept of self-presentation and its two dimensions: frontstage and backstage (Goffman, 1959). Frontstage self-presentation refers to how individuals present them-selves in public settings, while backstage self-presentation encompasses private behaviors. This framework can serve as a valuable lens to understand how teenagers portray themselves on social media.

In social media, frontstage self-presentation among teenagers involves carefully crafting and projecting a desired image or persona. Individuals utilize these platforms to share content that highlights their achievements, interests, and relationships, seeking social approval and attention from their peers (Davis, 2014). Conversely, backstage self-presentation on social media involves more intimate or personal expressions, typically shared through private channels to maintain privacy (Binns, 2013). Some teenagers may even adopt anonymous accounts or pseudonyms to engage in behaviors that deviate from their public persona.

The ways in which teenagers utilize frontstage and backstage self-presentation on social media vary based on their social context and peer group norms (e.g., Joanna & Stephanie, 2019; Rousseau, 2021; Nor & Fuat, 2021). While some prioritize self-expression and self-promotion, others seek social connection and validation from their peers with the hope to avoid digital shame (King, 2020).

The "self" is shaped by the gaze of "others," and shame arises when we become aware of this connection, as Sartre (1943) vividly depicts this experience in his work *Being and Nothingness*. Shame and shaming play a crucial role in maintaining social order and inequality, as they are linked to social status, poverty, appearance, and academic performance. Digital shame conflicts reflect broader social tensions, particularly in contexts where presentation and concealment are crucial for success and acceptance (King, 2020).

For example, Joanna and Stephanie (2019) pointed out that the feeling of being watched and evaluated by an "imaginary audience" leads young adolescents to seek more peer approval to avoid shame. Through focus group interviews with fifty-one middle school and high school students in the United States, Joanna and Stephanie (2019) identified that appearing interesting, likable, and attractive are main concerns for the participants to present themselves favorably to their peers and imaginary audience.

Similarly, Rousseau (2021) surveyed 949 Belgian adolescents on their selfie-taking and posting behaviors. Findings showed that increased exposure to appearance-focused media is linked to greater engagement in selfie-related activities (such as taking and posting selfies), as well as a higher level of investment in and editing the selfies. This connection is influenced by the internalization of thin or athletic ideals and the tendency to compare one's appearance with others on social media. Moreover, Van Ouytsel (2020) found a higher likelihood of older adolescents posting sexually suggestive images on Instagram, with girls demonstrating a significantly higher tendency for self-sexualized posts compared to boys.

Nor and Fuat (2021) examined 200 images of teenagers and emerging adults in Malaysia using a visual content analysis technique. The findings suggested that image editing tools and applications were used to present themselves as attractive and to receive good compliments from their friends.

In addition, adolescents tended to capture *close-up shots*, focusing on eyes and faces, more frequently than young adults, as they seek to convey a sense of intimacy and closeness with their imaginary audience. However, the authors did not find any pictures that indicated a desire to appear sexy and attractive, contrary to the study by Herring and Kapidzic (2015) conducted with teenagers in the United States. Nor and Fuat (2021) interpreted this finding as an influence of the cultural and religious values of Malaysia.

In a similar vein, the study of Korkmazer et al. (2020) emphasizes the significance of cultural discourses on young people's self-presentations on Instagram. The scholars aimed to understand how young people perceive gender, reputation, and sexual morality online through self-presentations on Instagram. Findings suggested that a neoliberal narrative that encourages subjects "to create and express a version of themselves that is marketable and creative while emphasizing the importance of emotionality and authentic experiences" was dominant in fifty-seven young participants' visual collages (thirteen and twenty years old).

In summary, self-presentation involves employing strategies to shape an impression of oneself by managing personal information in order to portray a desired self-image (Goffman, 1959). The available academic literature from different geographies and cultures provides us with insight into how self-presentation, peer influences, and exposure to dominant culture co-construct the standards of beauty and other normative subject positions for adolescents in the digital sphere.

SELF-DISCLOSURE THEORY IN DIGITAL COMMUNICATION

A key framework for understanding adolescents' behavior in computer-mediated communication is Self-Disclosure Theory. This theory, rooted in social psychology, involves sharing personal information—such as thoughts, feelings, and experiences—with others (Pang, 2024). When reciprocated, self-disclosure can foster intimacy, enhance satisfaction in friendships, and contribute to relational growth (Gibbs et al., 2006).

Self-Disclosure Theory has been applied to explore motivations and characteristics of disclosure on platforms like Instagram and online dating apps (Maharani, 2024; Catellya et al., 2023). For instance, Maharani and Febriana (2023) analyzed how Instagram Stories serve as a medium for self-disclosure. Their qualitative descriptive study focused on a celebrity's Instagram Stories, particularly themes related to fashion and makeup. The findings revealed that these stories blend personal and professional content, helping to connect with followers, enhance personal branding, and secure endorsements (Maharani &

Febriana, 2023). This underscores the importance of social media stories for connection and validation.

In a similar vein, the study by Gibbs et al. (2006) investigated the role of self-disclosure in online dating relationships using a sample of Match.com members. It examined how anticipated future face-to-face interaction influences online self-disclosure and perceived success in online dating. The findings highlighted that individuals who expect future face-to-face meetings tend to disclose more personal information online.

Additionally, Hossain et al. (2023) explored the impact of self-disclosure on Facebook on subjective well-being. This study, involving 244 respondents from Bangladesh, aimed to identify factors influencing self-disclosure and its effects on well-being. The findings showed that social influence, enjoyment, and frequent social media use encourage individuals to share personal information. This self-disclosure enhances social support, thereby improving overall well-being. Particularly during challenging times, such as the COVID-19 pandemic, sharing personal experiences on platforms like Facebook can strengthen social connections and improve mental health.

The above studies collectively highlight the significance of self-disclosure in digital communication. People can build stronger connections, improve their personal branding, and enhance their well-being on various social media platforms. However, it's important to be mindful of the potential negative consequences, such as overexposure and potential privacy violations.

THE FUNHOUSE MIRROR: PSYCHOLOGICAL NEGATIVE OUTCOMES

As we examined in the previous section, self-presentation on social media is a common aspect of adolescent life. However, the pressure to conform to idealized standards of appearance, behavior, and values can create a distorted sense of reality, both for the individual and for the wider community. This is where *the Funhouse Mirror allegory* comes into play—a metaphor that describes how social media can create a distorted reflection of reality.

Research shows that social media use is strongly associated with a range of negative outcomes for teenagers, including perceived anxiety, stress, depression, aggression, and poor self-esteem (Hjetland et al., 2021; Walton & Rizzolo, 2022; Jabbar et al., 2022; Winstone et al., 2022; Keles et al., 2020; Burnette et al., 2017). This is because social media platforms can create a highly filtered and manipulated version of reality that is often unrealistic and unattainable. The pressure to conform to these standards can be overwhelming, leading to feelings of inadequacy, loneliness, isolation, and cyberbullying (Popat & Tarrant, 2023).

The literature also informs us that being exposed to bullying on social media can have detrimental effects on an individual's mental well-being and overall health. The phenomenon known as "cyberbullying," which encompasses actions like name-calling and public humiliation, has been found to induce anxiety among teenagers (Calancie et al., 2017). Adolescents expressed the belief that, in certain instances, social media could potentially contribute to feelings of depression and, in severe cases, even lead to suicide (O'Reilly, 2020).

EMILY'S CASE: DIGITAL SELF-HARM

Meet Emily, a sixteen-year-old high school student who often posts photos showcasing her glamorous lifestyle—beach vacations, trendy outfits, and outings with friends at popular cafes. She frequently shares snapshots from concerts, joyous family gatherings, and her favorite desserts, like the best tiramisu from a chic local bakery. Her social media presence paints a picture of a popular, happy, and flawless life.

But behind this online persona, Emily has a secret. She has anonymously created three accounts to post cruel comments about herself. Disguised as various fictitious people, she attacks her own looks, intelligence, family, and worth. Strangely, Emily finds a twisted sense of satisfaction in the concern and sympathy these hurtful comments elicit from her friends and followers. She craves the attention and the perception that she's strong enough to handle such negativity. However, this harmful behavior is taking a serious toll on her mental health, trapping her in a destructive cycle of self-loathing and the need for external validation.

Emine's above hypothetical case serves as an illustration of an increasingly prevalent and new form of cyberbullying known as *digital self-harm*, *self-cyberbullying*, *self-trolling*, or *fictitious online victimization*. This phenomenon entails the act of anonymously or pseudonymously posting harmful or negative content about oneself on the internet and social media platforms, as outlined by Meldrum et al. (2022). The primary motivations behind this behavior among teenagers include making fun, demonstrating resilience, seeking sympathy and attention from others, and seeking reassurance of friendship (Pacheco et al., 2019).

Research highlights a link between digital self-harm and experiences of bullying. Individuals who have been bullied, whether in person or online, were notably more likely to admit engaging in digital self-harm (Patchin & Hinduja, 2017). For instance, a study conducted with Florida youth uncovered a strong association between being a victim of bullying and engaging in digital self-harm. This means that individuals who experience bullying are more likely to engage in the harmful practice of posting negative information about themselves online while maintaining anonymity or using a different identity (Meldrum et al., 2022).

Interestingly, another study involving high school students from Florida suggests that inadequate sleep may be linked to digital self-harm behavior (Semenza et al., 2022). The authors of the study recommended that professionals and healthcare providers should have conversations about digital self-harm with adolescents and their parents, particularly when adolescents are facing issues related to sleep deprivation and depressive symptoms.

The existing empirical literature highlights the significance of family dynamics in teenagers' engagement in digital self-harm behaviors. Research indicates that a weak attachment to parents significantly increases the likelihood of participating in digital self-harm, primarily through the mediation of negative emotions experienced by adolescents (Loes, 2022).

Another recent study conducted by Erreygers et al. (2022) shed light on the relationships between self-digital bullying and various aspects of well-being. The findings revealed significant negative associations between self-digital bullying and individuals' self-esteem, subjective well-being, and life satisfaction. In other words, those who experienced self-digital bullying reported lower levels of self-esteem, subjective well-being, and life satisfaction. Additionally, the study identified a positive association between self-digital bullying and narcissism. This suggests that individuals who engage in self-digital bullying may exhibit higher levels of narcissistic traits.

To summarize, the examination of current literature shows that digital self-harm is a new and concerning phenomenon. Future studies should investigate the psychological mechanisms underlying digital self-harm, exploring factors such as low self-esteem, negative self-perception, and the need for validation. Understanding these motivations can inform targeted prevention strategies and therapeutic interventions. Additionally, examining the role of peer relationships and social dynamics in digital self-harm can provide insights into social influences and guide the development of interventions that foster positive online peer relationships. Longitudinal research is needed to understand the long-term consequences of digital self-harm on mental health and well-being, identifying protective factors and effective coping strategies. Interventions and prevention efforts should be developed and evaluated to address digital self-harm effectively. Future research could explore the efficacy of educational programs, counseling interventions, and digital literacy campaigns. Furthermore, studying the qualitative perspectives and experiences of individuals who have experienced digital self-harm can provide valuable insights into successful intervention strategies to foster a healthier online environment for adolescents.

CONCLUSION

The impact of social media on teen self-presentation is multilayered. Social media platforms provide teenagers with an opportunity to present themselves in ways that are different from their offline selves. From an educational psychology and technology perspective, it is important to recognize the potential risks and benefits of social media use for teenagers and to develop strategies to help them navigate these platforms safely and responsibly. This includes promoting digital literacy skills, encouraging critical thinking and self-reflection, and fostering positive social connections and support networks.

"REFLECT AND REFRAME" FOR ADULTS

1. How does your online persona differ from your offline self, and what drives these differences?
2. In what ways can social media platforms contribute to both positive and negative mental health outcomes for teenagers?
3. What are the potential benefits and risks of using anonymity on social media for self-presentation and self-expression?

4. How do cultural and peer influences shape the ways teenagers present themselves online?
5. What strategies can be implemented to mitigate the negative effects of social media on teenagers' mental health and promote healthier online behaviors?

"REFLECT AND REFRAME" FOR KIDS

1. How is the "you" on the internet different from the "you" in real life, and why do you think that happens?
2. How can using social media (like Instagram or TikTok) make teenagers feel happy or sad?
3. What are the good and bad things about using fake names when you share about yourself?
4. How do your friends and family make you act on the internet?
5. What can we do to help people feel better and stay safe when they use social media?

REFERENCES

Binns, A. (2013). Facebook's ugly sisters: Anonymity and abuse on formspring and ask.fm. *Media Education Research Journal, 4*(1), 27.

Burnette, C. B., Kwitowski, M. A., & Mazzeo, S. E. (2017). I don't need people to tell me I'm pretty on social media: A qualitative study of social media and body image in early adolescent girls. *Body Image, 23*, 114–125.

Calancie, O., Ewing, L., Narducci, L., Horgan, S., & Khalid-Khan, S. (2017). Exploring how social networking sites impact youth with anxiety: A qualitative study of Facebook stressors among adolescents with an anxiety disorder diagnosis. *Cyberpsychology: Journal of Psychosocial Research on Cyberspace, 11*(4). https://doi.org/10.5817/cp2017-4-2

Davis, K. (2012). Friendship 2.0: Adolescents' experiences of belonging and self-disclosure online. *Journal of Adolescence, 35*(6), 1527–1536.

Davis, K. (2014). Youth identities in a digital age: The anchoring role of friends in young people's approaches to online identity expression. In A. Bennett & B. Robards (Eds.), *Mediated youth cultures* (pp. 11–25). Springer.

Erreygers, S., Symons, M., Vandebosch, H., & Pabian, S. (2022). Fictitious online victimization: Exploration and creation of a measurement instrument. *New Media & Society, 24*(1), 156–177.

Gibbs, J., Ellison, N., & Heino, R. (2006). Self-presentation in online personals. *Communication Research, 33*(2), 152–177. https://doi.org/10.1177/0093650205285368

Giletta, M., Choukas-Bradley, S., Maes, M., Linthicum, K., Card, N., & Prinstein, M. (2021). A meta-analysis of longitudinal peer influence effects in childhood and adolescence. *Psychological Bulletin, 147*(7), 719–747.

Goffman, E. (1959). *The presentation of self in everyday life*. New York: Doubleday.

Herring, S. C., & Kapidzic, S. (2015). Teens, gender, and self-presentation in social media. *International Encyclopedia of Social and Behavioral Sciences, 2*, 1–16.

Hjetland, G. J., Schønning, V., Hella, R. T., Veseth, M., & Skogen, J. C. (2021). How do Norwegian adolescents experience the role of social media in relation to mental health and well-being: A qualitative study. *BMC Psychology, 9*(1), 78.

Jabbar, J., Dharmarajan, S., Raveendranathan, R. P., Syamkumar, D., & Jasseer, A. (2022). Influence of social media on adolescent mental health. *International Journal of English Literature and Social Sciences (IJELS), 7*(1), 72–76.

Juwita, E., Effendi, A. Z., & Pandin, M. G. R. (2021). The effect of anonymity on Twitter towards its users based on Derek Parfit's personal identity theory. OSF Preprints. https://doi.org/10.31219/osf.io/pc4se

Kapidzic, S., & Herring, S. C. (2014). Race, gender, and self-presentation in teen profile photographs. *New Media & Society, 17*(6), 958–976. https://doi.org10.1177/1461444813520301

Keles, B., McCrae, N., & Grealish, A. (2020). A systematic review: The influence of social media on depression, anxiety and psychological distress in adolescents. *International Journal of Adolescence and Youth, 25*(1), 79–93.

King, V. (2020). "Lots of people pretend..." Shame conflicts in an age of digital self-presentation and point-scoring. *Beijing International Review of Education, 2*(3), 388–402.

Korkmazer, B., De Ridder, S., & Van Bauwel, S. (2021). The visual digital self: A discourse theoretical analysis of young people's negotiations on gender, reputation and sexual morality online. *Digest Journal of Diversity and Gender Studies, 8*(1), 22–40.

Loes, C. N. (2022). Parental attachment and digital self-harm. *Deviant Behavior, 44*(3), 1–14.

Maharani, A. (2024). Use of Instagram stories feature as self disclosure media on @ azkhategar account. *Jurnal Spektrum Komunikasi, 12*(1), 124–134. https://doi.org /10.37826/spektrum.v12i1.703

Marcia, J. E. (1980). Identity in adolescence. In J. Adelson (Ed.), *Handbook of adolescent psychology* (pp. 159–187). Hoboken, NJ: John Wiley & Sons.

Meldrum, R. C., Patchin, J. W., Young, J. T., & Hinduja, S. (2022). Bullying victimization, negative emotions, and digital self-harm: Testing a theoretical model of indirect effects. *Deviant Behavior, 43*(3), 303–321.

Nor, N. F. M., & Fuat, N. H. B. M. (2021). Visual analysis of self-presentation of teenagers and emerging adults on Facebook. *Indonesian Journal of Applied Linguistics, 10*(3), 707–718.

O'reilly, M. (2020). Social media and adolescent mental health: The good, the bad and the ugly. *Journal of Mental Health, 29*(2), 200–206.

Pacheco, E., Melhuish, N., & Fiske, J. (2019). *Digital self-harm: Prevalence, motivations and outcomes for teens who cyberbully themselves.* Wellington, New Zealand.

Pang, T. (2024). Self-concept clarity and loneliness among college students: The chain-mediating effect of fear of negative evaluation and self-disclosure. *Behavioral Sciences, 14*(3), 194. https://doi.org/10.3390/bs14030194

Patchin, J. W., & Hinduja, S. (2017). Digital self-harm among adolescents. *Journal of Adolescent Health, 61*(6), 761–766.

Popat, A., & Tarrant, C. (2023). Exploring adolescents' perspectives on social media and mental health and well-being–A qualitative literature review. *Clinical Child Psychology and Psychiatry, 28*(1), 323–337.

Rousseau, A. (2021). Adolescents' selfie-activities and idealized online self-presentation: An application of the sociocultural model. *Body Image, 36*, 16–26. https:// doi-org.proxyiub.uits.iu.edu/10.1016/j.bodyim.2020.10.005

Ruppel, E., Gross, C., Stoll, A., Peck, B., Allen, M., & Kim, S. (2016). Reflecting on connecting: Meta-analysis of differences between computer-mediated and face-to-face self-disclosure. *Journal of Computer-Mediated Communication, 22*(1), 18–34. https://doi.org/10.1111/jcc4.12179

Sartre, J. P. (1943). *Being and nothingness.* New York: Washington Square Press.

Semenza, D. C., Meldrum, R. C., Testa, A., & Jackson, D. B. (2022). Sleep duration, depressive symptoms, and digital self-harm among adolescents. *Child and Adolescent Mental Health, 27*(2), 103–110.

Tokunaga, R. S. (2010). Following you home from school: A critical review and synthesis of research on cyberbullying victimization. *Computers in Human Behavior*, *26*(3), 277–287.

Van Ouytsel, J., Walrave, M., Ojeda, M., Del Rey, R., & Ponnet, K. (2020). Adolescents' sexy self-presentation on Instagram: An investigation of their posting behavior using a prototype willingness model perspective. *International Journal of Environmental Research and Public Health*, *17*(21), 8106.

Walther, J. B. (1996). Computer-mediated communication: Impersonal, interpersonal, and hyperpersonal interaction. *Communication Research, 23*(1), 1–43.

Walton, B., & Rizzolo, D. (2022). The effects of social media on adolescent mental health. *Pediatrics and Neonatal Nursing – Open Journal*, *8*(2), 43–47. https://doi.org/10.17140/PNNOJ-8-138

Winstone, L., Mars, B., Haworth, C. M., Heron, J., & Kidger, J. (2022). Adolescent social media user types and their mental health and well-being: Results from a longitudinal survey of 13–14 year olds in the United Kingdom. *JCPP Advances*, *2*(2), e12071.

Chapter 2

Cyberdating Abuse among Teens

LEARNING OBJECTIVES

Upon completion of this chapter, you will be able to:

1. Discuss various forms of cyberdating abuse and their impact on victims' emotional and mental well-being.
2. Identify the role of Attachment Theory and how attachment styles influence behaviors in digital relationships.
3. Develop strategies to recognize, prevent, and address cyberdating abuse in adolescent relationships, promoting healthy and respectful interactions.

CYBERDATING ABUSE

Meet Sarah and Jake, two high school students who have been dating for seven months.

As their relationship progresses, Jake becomes increasingly possessive and suspicious of Sarah's interactions with other friends on social media platforms. He constantly monitors her online activity, keeping a close eye on her comments, likes, and even private messages. He insists that she should always be available to chat, respond to his messages promptly, and immediately acknowledge his posts. He becomes upset if Sarah takes longer than a few minutes to reply or if she spends time engaging with other friends on the platform. Jake's controlling behavior escalates as he manipulates Sarah into exchanging passwords, claiming that it is a sign of trust and commitment in their relationship.

Jake's demands don't stop there. He pressures Sarah to unfriend or block male friends and restricts her from posting pictures that don't include him. If Sarah ever fails to comply, Jake accuses her of not loving him enough or hiding something. Additionally, Jake starts dictating what Sarah should wear, arguing that certain outfits might attract unwanted attention from other boys. He insists on knowing her whereabouts at all times, even demanding she share her location through a tracking app. If Sarah ever tries to assert her independence or question Jake's behavior, he turns the conversation around, making her feel guilty for not being a supportive girlfriend.

Sarah, eager to please Jake and maintain their relationship, begins to feel trapped and suffocated by his constant surveillance. She experiences anxiety whenever she receives notifications on social media, fearing that Jake may become angry or accuse her of being unfaithful or disinterested in their relationship. This constant pressure and emotional turmoil impact Sarah's self-esteem and overall well-being.

The above hypothetical case illustrates jealousy and controlling behaviors manifesting through the use of social media. Sarah's romantic experience spirals into an emotionally harmful dynamic, eroding trust and individual autonomy, called cyberdating abuse (Van Ouytsel et al., 2016). Violence among teenagers represents a worldwide public health issue (UNESCO, 2017). According to Zweig et al. (2014), cyberdating abuse, a common yet often overlooked issue, refers to the harmful behaviors that occur within romantic relationships facilitated by digital platforms. It encompasses various forms of digital violence, including harassment, stalking, impersonation, controlling behaviors, and nonconsensual sharing of intimate images (Borrajo et al., 2015).

Romantic relationships hold a significant place in the lives of adolescents, influencing their emotional growth and social development. In the contemporary digital era, where technology has become deeply ingrained in their daily interactions, it is imperative to examine the correlation between technology and the prevalence of unhealthy behaviors within these relationships. While technology undoubtedly presents numerous opportunities for learning and positive interaction among young individuals, empirical studies have shed light on the potential of technology to both facilitate and amplify negative dynamics within adolescent dating relationships.

Researchers have highlighted the significance of understanding cyberdating violence to address its adverse effects on teens' emotional well-being and mental health. Current research shows that adolescents who engage in physical, psychological, or cyberbullying are more inclined to be involved in both perpetrating and experiencing cyberdating abuse as well, such as controlling, stalking, and image sharing (Yahner et al., 2015). The most frequently cited methods of exerting control over a partner were sharing passwords and monitoring profiles (Van Ouytsel et al., 2016). According to a study of Sanchez et al.

(2021) conducted in Spain, using fictional WhatsApp scenarios, adolescents perceived private cyber aggression as more frequent but less severe compared to public cyber aggressions. In the examination of gender differences concerning cyber aggression in digital relationships, it was observed that girls reported a higher prevalence and greater severity of cyberdating aggression compared to boys. Similarly, in another research project involving teenagers with dating experience, it was discovered that girls and boys had distinct perspectives on digital monitoring (Lucero et al., 2014), where girls viewed digital monitoring, surveillance, and password sharing as acceptable relationship actions driven by the desire to safeguard and sustain a dating relationship. Sanchez et al. (2021) recommend developing prevention programs tailored to address the social nature of dating aggression on online platforms.

In another recent study conducted in Canada, Wallace et al. (2023) discuss the prevalence and factors associated with cyberdating violence (cyber-DV) victimization among adolescent girls in Quebec, Canada. The study reveals that a significant proportion (63.3 percent) of adolescent girls reported experiencing at least one form of cyber-DV. The authors indicate the connection between online and offline DV and emphasize the development of universal school programs to address both forms of DV.

TRUST AND ATTACHMENT THEORY

Attachment Theory (Bowlby, 1973) offers a helpful way to explain how the attachment patterns adolescents develop in their early relationships can affect how they behave and feel in both online and offline romantic situations (Reed et al., 2016). This theory was initially developed by British psychologist John Bowlby in the mid-twentieth century. Attachment theory has significantly contributed to our understanding of human development, interpersonal relationships, and psychological well-being.

At its core, Attachment Theory posits that humans have an innate need for attachment and connection with others, particularly during infancy and childhood. This need for attachment is considered a fundamental and biologically based human drive, akin to the need for food and shelter. The primary caregiver, usually the mother or father, plays a crucial role in satisfying this attachment need by providing emotional support, care, and a secure base for the child to explore the world.

It categorizes individuals into different attachment styles based on their early caregiving experiences. The most commonly recognized attachment styles are secure, anxious-ambivalent, avoidant, and disorganized (Mallon, 2008). These styles reflect how individuals perceive and approach relationships based on their early attachment experiences.

Individuals with a secure attachment style tend to have had consistent, responsive, and emotionally available caregivers during childhood. They develop a positive view of themselves and others, leading to healthy, trusting, and fulfilling relationships in adulthood (Ainsworth, 1979). Anxious-ambivalent attachment classifies people who experience anxiety when relationships potentially end because they are afraid of losing a connection with a particular individual. They tend to feel concerned about abandonment, particularly during challenging or uncertain circumstances. Next, the avoidant attachment dimension refers to individuals who perceive that others are rejecting them in their relationships, leading them to be unwilling to form close connections (Ainsworth, 1979). Finally, disorganized attachment style arises from inconsistent and often abusive caregiving. Individuals with disorganized attachment may have difficulty regulating their emotions and struggle with forming stable relationships in adulthood.

Some studies examined the relationship between social media platforms and attachment style in romantic and other relationships. For example, the study "Predicting Facebook Jealousy in Romantic Relationships: Further Support for Attachment Style and Trust" by researchers Simran Hira and Manpal Singh Bhogal (2020) researched the role of attachment styles and relationship quality in predicting Facebook jealousy. Conducted with 124 participants in heterosexual romantic relationships, the study found that individuals with high attachment anxiety experienced higher levels of Facebook jealousy. Conversely, those with low attachment avoidance and low trust also showed increased Facebook jealousy. The study highlighted that anxious attachment, characterized by fear of abandonment, leads to frequent partner monitoring online, increasing jealousy. Meanwhile, avoidantly attached individuals, who typically maintain emotional distance, experienced lower jealousy.

Also, Santoro et al. (2024) studied attachment styles, mentalizing capacities, and levels of problematic social media use (PSMU) such as excessive time spent online, neglect of offline responsibilities, and emotional dependency on social media interactions. The findings indicate that individuals with secure and dismissing attachment styles are less likely to engage in PSMU, while those with preoccupied and fearful attachment styles are more prone to problematic use. The study highlights that failures in mentalization, the ability to understand and interpret one's own and others' mental states, mediate these relationships, suggesting that improving mentalization could mitigate PSMU. Specifically, secure attachment promotes better mentalizing, reducing PSMU.

Finally, the study conducted by Eichenberg et al. (2024) aims to explore the relationship between attachment styles, mental distress, personality traits, and social media addiction among college students in Vienna. Using an online survey, the study employed various scales to assess social media addiction, attachment styles, mental distress, and personality traits.

Key findings include that 22.7 percent of participants were identified as addicted to social media. These individuals displayed higher levels of neuroticism, depression, anxiety, and somatization compared to their non-addicted peers. Notably, students with an ambivalent closed attachment style—characterized by anxiety, dependency, and a fear of abandonment—were more likely to be addicted to social media.

OTHER FORMS OF CYBERDATING ABUSE

The review of the literature suggests various forms of cyberdating abuse, some of which may initially appear innocent. However, these behaviors can have profound and damaging effects on victims (Table 2.1).

Table 2.1 Different Forms of Cyberdating Violence

Threats of Revenge Porn	Manipulating Online Identity	Public Shaming on Social Media	Excessive Texting or Calling
Weaponized Emojis and GIFs	Spreading False Information via Social Media	Threats to End the Relationship	Manipulating Group Chats
Sexting Pressure	Emotional Manipulation	Excessive Complaints about Friends	Tracking Location without Consent
Gaslighting	Dependency on Digital Communication	Doxing	Digital Monitoring

One particularly malicious form is threats of *revenge porn*, where abusers threaten to share intimate images or videos to maintain control (O'Connor et al., 2018). Additionally, the seemingly harmless use of *emojis and GIFs* can be weaponized to convey sarcasm or passive-aggressive messages, adding to the emotional distress (Karim et al., 2022). *Sexting pressure* is another one that refers to coercing teens into sending explicit content, which can lead to anxiety and shame if shared without consent (Laird et al., 2021). Abusers might *manipulate their partner's online identity*, forcing changes in usernames or profile pictures to erase individuality. *Spreading false* information via social media can further damage reputations and relationships (Brod & Vangelisti, 2017).

Additionally, as discussed, *emotional manipulation* and *sending mixed signals* through digital platforms can significantly destabilize a partner's emotional well-being. *Fostering a dependency* on constant digital communication can lead to anxiety when contact is interrupted. Tactics such as *public shaming* on social media, threats to end the relationship, and excessive complaints about friends are used to exert control and create conflict (Betts et al., 2017; Nazir & Thabassum, 2021; Scheithauer et al., 2021).

Finally, *excessive texting or calling* creates an obligation to respond immediately, fostering anxiety. *Manipulating group chats* to spread rumors or isolate the victim, *tracking someone's location* through technology without consent, and gaslighting, which involves psychological manipulation to make victims doubt their own perceptions, are all tactics used in cyberdating abuse. Additionally, *doxing*, which publicly reveals private information, adds another layer of intimidation and control.

CONCLUSION

In conclusion, the pervasive and subtle nature of cyberdating abuse reveals how digital platforms can amplify harmful behaviors in romantic relationships. From threats of revenge porn and digital monitoring to emotional manipulation and public shaming, the spectrum of abuse is broad and deeply impactful. Moreover, attachment theory can help us understand how early relationship patterns influence these behaviors, highlighting the need for targeted interventions. Teaching young individuals about these forms of cyberdating violence is essential to fostering healthy, respectful relationships.

"REFLECT AND REFRAME" FOR ADULTS

1. How do you feel about the "seen" feature on Facebook and other social media platforms? Does knowing someone has read your message but hasn't replied change your perception of the interaction?
2. Reflect on a time when you felt pressured to share your social media passwords or location with someone. How did this request make you feel, and what impact did it have on your relationship?
3. Has anyone ever converted your image into a meme or used an emoji to mock you? How did this affect your emotions and the dynamics of your social interactions?
4. Have you ever found yourself going through your romantic partner's friend list and checking each person one by one? What motivated you to do this, and how did it affect your trust and feelings in the relationship?
5. Consider the ways in which digital monitoring can influence trust in a relationship. How would you address a situation where you felt your online activities were being excessively monitored by a partner?

"REFLECT AND REFRAME" FOR KIDS

1. How do you feel when you see that someone saw your message but didn't answer? Does it make you happy or sad?
2. Has someone ever asked for your secret password or where you are? How did it make you feel?
3. Has anyone ever made fun of a picture of you or used a funny face to tease you? How did it make you feel?
4. Have you ever looked at who your friend is talking to on the computer? Why did you do that, and how did it make you feel?
5. How would you feel if someone was always watching what you do on the computer? What would you say to them?

REFERENCES

Betts, L. R., Gkimitzoudis, A., Spenser, K. A., & Baguley, T. (2017). Examining the roles young people fulfill in five types of cyberbullying. *Journal of Social and Personal Relationships, 34*(7), 1080–1098.

Borrajo, E., Gámez-Guadix, M., Pereda, N., & Calvete, E. (2015). The development and validation of the cyber dating abuse questionnaire among young couples. *Computers in Human Behavior, 48*, 358–365.

Bowlby, J. (1973). *Attachment and loss: Vol. 2. Separation: Anxiety and anger.* New York: Basic Books

Brody, N., & Vangelisti, A. L. (2017). Cyberbullying: Topics, strategies, and sex differences. *Computers in Human Behavior, 75*, 739–748.

Eichenberg, C., Schneider, R., & Rumpl, H. (2024). Social media addiction: associations with attachment style, mental distress, and personality. *BMC Psychiatry, 24*(1), 278. https://doi.org/10.1186/s12888-024-05709-z

Hira, S., & Bhogal, M. (2020). Predicting Facebook jealousy in romantic relationships: Further support for attachment style and trust. *Current Psychology, 41*(9), 6166–6169. https://doi.org/10.1007/s12144-020-01115-2

Karim, M. R., Dey, S. K., Islam, T., Shajalal, M., & Chakravarthi, B. R. (2022, November). Multimodal hate speech detection from Bengali memes and texts. In *International conference on speech and language technologies for low-resource languages* (pp. 293–308). Cham: Springer International Publishing.

Laird, J. J., Klettke, B., Clancy, E. M., & Fuelscher, I. (2021). Relationships between coerced sexting and differentiation of self: An exploration of protective factors. *Sexes, 2*(4), 468–482. https://doi.org/10.3390/sexes2040037

Lucero, J. L., Weisz, A. N., Smith-Darden, J., & Lucero, S. M. (2014). Exploring gender differences: Socially interactive technology use/abuse among dating teens. *Affilia, 29*(4), 478–491.

Nazir, T., & Thabassum, L. (2021). Cyberbullying: Definition, types, effects, related factors and precautions to be taken during COVID-19 pandemic. *The International Journal of Indian Psychology, 9*(4), 480–491.

O'Connor, K. W., Drouin, M., Davis, J., & Thompson, H (2018). Cyberbullying, revenge porn and the mid-sized university: Victim characteristics, prevalence and students' knowledge of university policy and reporting procedures. *Higher Education Quarterly, 72*(4), 344–359. https://doi.org/10.1111/hequ.12171

Reed, L. A., Tolman, R. M., Ward, L. M., & Safyer, P. (2016). Keeping tabs: Attachment anxiety and electronic intrusion in high school dating relationships. *Computers in Human Behavior, 58*, 259–268.

Santoro, G. (2024). Insecure minds through the looking glass: The mediating role of mentalization in the relationships between adult attachment styles and problematic social media use. *International Journal of Environmental Research and Public Health, 21*(3), 255. https://doi.org/10.3390/ijerph21030255

Scheithauer, H., Schultze-Krumbholz, A., Pfetsch, J., & Hess, M. (2021). Types of cyberbullying. In K. S. Peter & O. N. James (Eds.), *The Wiley Blackwell handbook of bullying: A comprehensive and international review of research and intervention*, vol 1 (pp. 120–138). London: Wiley-Blackwell.

UNESCO. (2017). School violence and bullying: Global status report. UNESCO Publishing.

Van Ouytsel, J., Ponnet, K., & Walrave, M. (2016). Cyber dating abuse victimization among secondary school students from a lifestyle-routine activities theory perspective. *Journal of Interpersonal Violence, 33*(17), 2767–2776. Online ahead of print. https://doi.org/10.1177/0886260516629390

Van Ouytsel, J., Van Gool, E., Walrave, M., Ponnet, K., & Peeters, E. (2016). Exploring the role of social networking sites within adolescent romantic relationships and dating experiences. *Computers in Human Behavior, 55*, 76–86. http://doi.org.lib-e2.lib.ttu.edu/10.1016/j.chb.2015.08.042

Wallace, A., Langevin, R., & Hébert, M. (2023). An analysis of risk and protective factors associated with cyber-dating violence victimization of adolescent girls: An ecological perspective. *Journal of Child & Adolescent Trauma, 16*(8), 1–13.

Yahner, J., Dank, M., Zweig, J. M., & Lachman, P. (2015). The co-occurrence of physical and cyber dating violence and bullying among teens. *Journal of Interpersonal Violence, 30*(7), 1079–1089. http://doi.org.lib-e2.lib.ttu.edu/10.1177/0886260514540324

Zweig, J., Lachman, P., Yahner, J., & Dank, M. (2014). Correlates of cyber dating abuse among teens. *Journal of Youth and Adolescence, 43*, 1306–1321. https://doi.org/10.1007/s10964-013-0047-x

Chapter 3

Online Games and Cyberbullying

LEARNING OBJECTIVES

Upon completion of this chapter, you will be able to:

1. Identify the connection between online gaming environments and the prevalence of cyberbullying.
2. Discuss how anonymity and the competitive nature in online games contribute to bullying behavior.
3. Explore ethical dilemma types and the role of Social Exchange Theory in a digital context.
4. Discuss common acronyms and slang used by teenagers in online gaming to better monitor and support their interactions.

In December 2023, a tragic incident from Texas was reported, where a child died by suicide during an online gaming session following relentless cyberbullying. The victim, still wearing a gaming headset, was found at home, having been driven to this extreme by harassment from a peer in Michigan. The Michigan teen, who convinced the victim to commit suicide, has been placed on probation for aiding the act and harassment causing death (News Source).

Reflecting on this heartbreaking event, it's hard not to draw parallels to the *Lord of the Flies* movie, where children left to govern themselves on an island descend into chaos and brutality. Online gaming spaces can similarly become unregulated environments where civility and morality are dictated by the players, often with devastating outcomes. This incident reminds us of the importance of oversight and guidance in these virtual worlds.

The connection between online games and cyberbullying stems from several inherent factors within gaming environments. For example, the anonymity afforded by avatars and usernames can encourage individuals to engage in bullying behaviors they might avoid in face-to-face interactions (McInroy & Mishna, 2017).

The competitive and violent nature of some online games often leads to heightened emotions and aggression, while the perceived lack of immediate consequences can foster a sense of freedom (Lam et al., 2013). Communication channels in games provide avenues for abusive messages and harassment, and the culture within some gaming communities can tolerate or even encourage toxic behavior (Kwak et al., 2025). Additionally, gender and perceived hostility and aggressive behavior due to the psychological distance further contribute to the prevalence of cyberbullying in online gaming (Yang, 2012).

ONLINE GAME CHATTING AND CYBERBULLYING

Current empirical research from various countries highlights the significant role of culture and societal norms in shaping the interpretation of cyberbullying. This results in inconsistencies regarding the perceived causes, contexts, and demographic factors associated with cyberbullying. Despite these variations, a common factor contributing to cyberbullying is the presence of online chatting with other gamers during gameplay. Players communicate in online games because these games are inherently social activities, whether they are cooperative, competitive, or designed primarily for socializing; talking helps achieve in-game objectives and fosters social interaction.

Social interactions in online gaming, especially in multiplayer games, greatly enhance the enjoyment of play. These interactions foster lifelong friendships and partnerships, allowing players to express themselves freely without the constraints of appearance, gender, sexuality, or age. Additionally, these games provide a space for teamwork, encouragement, and fun (Scott & Porter-Armstrong, 2013).

However, managing aggressive behavior that emerges from stressful situations in competitive online games, where players have little to no control, can be extremely challenging (Maldonado, 2016). Gamer aggression can negatively impact mood and relationships, persisting even after the gaming session ends (Kowert, 2020). Furthermore, constant harassment from toxic players can lead to depression among other participants (Smith, 2019).

For instance, in a study titled "There's a Fine Line between Trash-Talking and Cyberbullying," Kaye et al. (2022) investigated male youth's reflections on their adolescent online gaming experiences, particularly reflections on cyberbullying in a Western Canadian city. Participants were asked for the definition of cyberbullying from their own perspectives and acknowledged key concepts of cyberbullying such as anonymity, consistency, and intention to harm as presented in the following excerpt:

> There are these kinds of masks you talk behind, you don't talk face-to-face, they don't see you when you're talking. When you're talking to someone face-to-face, you look at the eyes of the person and you get intimidated or you think better of what you're doing. But if you're talking through a microphone without showing your face, you tend to be more irresponsible of what you say and how you say it. (Kaye et al., 2022, p. 433)

It is interesting that they believed cyberbullying rarely occurred in online gaming, contradicting existing research. In addition, trash-talking, the act of making boastful, insulting, or provocative statements, was generally seen as fun and a bonding experience, not intended to harm, and was distinguished from cyberbullying. However, trash-talking could escalate to cyberbullying if it violated unwritten rules or involved strangers. Participants viewed trash-talking as part of the social norms within certain gaming contexts and believed it should not be equated with cyberbullying unless it crossed specific boundaries.

In another study, AlJaffer et al. (2021) explored the impact of online video games on young Saudi gamers, focusing on the risk of developing depression due to cyberbullying. Conducted between October and December 2019, the research involved an anonymous online questionnaire distributed via social media, with 143 caregivers of young Saudi gamers participating through a random sampling method. Exclusion criteria included individuals with known psychiatric or neurological histories. The study found that cyberbullying was more common among older teens and young adults, slightly more prevalent in males than in females, and more frequent among those with chronic illnesses. Youth with divorced parents and those from lower-income families also reported higher rates of cyberbullying. A significant finding was that the presence of online game chatting was strongly associated with cyberbullying.

SAFETY TIPS FOR PARENTS

In-game chat differs by game, but common methods include built-in voice or text chat, quick chat with preset phrases, and platform messaging systems like PlayStation Network or Steam Friends & Chat. Players may also use non-verbal "ping" systems to alert others to items or hazards and external apps like Discord or WhatsApp for voice, video, or text communication. These chats can also extend outside the game to social media or other online forums.

The risks of in-game chat include interacting with strangers, such as adults, and encountering inappropriate or unmoderated conversations that may involve swearing or insults, like being called names for playing poorly. Additionally, players may be asked to move to private chats, where they could be pressured to share personal information or engage in risky behavior, such as being asked to trade in-game items for real-life money.

To help ensure your child's in-game chat is safe and appropriate, consider these practical steps recommended by the CEOP Education (2024):

- **Get Involved:** Play or watch your children play online games to see how they talk and interact with others and understand what you're comfortable with.
- **Talk Regularly:** For older children who may not want you to play with them, have regular conversations about the games they play and whom they talk to.
- **Use Controls:** Utilize family controls and in-game settings to manage, limit, or turn off chat features to ensure your child's interactions are appropriate.
- **Shared Spaces:** For younger children, keep gaming devices in common areas like the living room and use settings to limit screen time to help them manage their time better.
- **Encourage Reporting:** Teach your children to report inappropriate chat and to tell you if anything in the game makes them feel uncomfortable or worried.

When you see your teen's text messages or social media chats, you might often find yourself confused by the acronyms and abbreviations they use. These slang and acronyms can seem like an entirely new language. While you might know common phrases like "ASAP" (as soon as possible) and "FYI" (for your information), there are many more that parents should be aware of. Here are some selected terms to watch out for as compiled by Morin (2022):

PAW: Parents are watching.
POS: Parents over shoulder, or sometimes "piece of sh**" in certain contexts.
SOS: Someone over shoulder.
KPC: Keeping parents clueless.
AFK: Away from keyboard.
TDTM: Talk dirty to me.
TIME: Tears in my eyes.
143: I love you.
H8: Hate.
HAK: Hugs and kisses.

OC: Open crib (no parents will be home).

GHOST: To be ignored by someone, as if you're invisible; common in online dating.

DANK: Something very good.

OP: On Reddit and other forums, short for "original poster," the person who started a post or thread.

GNOC: Get naked on camera.

NIFOC: Naked in front of computer.

ASL: Age/sex/location.

FWB: Friends with benefits (friends who occasionally have casual sex).

FYEO or 4YEO: For your eyes only (may indicate explicit photos).

GYPO: Get your pants off.

IWSN: I want sex now.

LMIRL: Let's meet in real life.

NSFW: Not safe for work.

NOOB: A novice, new player, or inexperienced user.

Being familiar with these terms can be incredibly helpful for parents looking to get involved in their children's online gaming activities and chat behaviors.

NETIQUETTE AND ETHICAL DILEMMAS

Understanding the value-building processes of adolescents is essential for designing courses and educational materials that help them stay safe and make informed decisions throughout their lives.

Park et al. (2014) surveyed 1200 adolescents aged 12 to 15 years old in South Korea during April and May 2013 to understand the relationship between online activities and cyberbullying. The findings showed a significant link between the amount of time spent online and the occurrence of cyberbullying. Importantly, the study found that adolescents who spent more time studying online, practiced good online etiquette (netiquette), and communicated regularly with their parents were less likely to engage in cyberbullying. Factors such as age and location also played a role in cyberbullying behavior. For instance, younger adolescents within the twelve to fifteen age group were more involved in cyberbullying. Additionally, youth living in urban areas were more likely to participate in online bullying, as well as to encounter and become victims of such behavior.

Additionally, frequent use of the internet and social networking sites was associated with higher levels of cyberbullying. The authors emphasized the importance of parental involvement, discussing guidelines for proper online

Table 3.1 Ethical Dilemma Types, Descriptions, and Examples

Ethical Dilemma	Description	Examples
Truth vs. Loyalty	Choosing between maintaining personal integrity or staying faithful to friends, family, or community.	**Reporting a Friend:** A student discovers that their best friend is cyberbullying another classmate. Should they report the friend to school authorities (truth) or keep their friend's secret (loyalty)?
Individual vs. Group	Choosing between the interests of an individual or a few and those of a larger community.	**Group Assignment:** Should a student report bullying in a group project, knowing it might cause the group to fail?
Immediate vs. Future	Weighing immediate benefits against potential long-term advantages.	**Blocking the Bully:** Should someone block a cyberbully right away, which offers immediate relief, or document the behavior for a future case?
Justice vs. Compassion	Choosing between applying fair and strict consequences or showing empathy and offering support.	**Public Shaming:** Should a cyberbully be publicly exposed (justice), or should efforts be made to privately address and educate them (compassion)?

behavior and educational activities that encourage online netiquette and dilemma training.

An online ethical dilemma is a situation in a digital or internet-based context where a person must make a difficult decision between conflicting ethical principles or guidelines, with no option providing a completely ethical outcome. These dilemmas often arise due to the unique characteristics of online environments, such as anonymity, instant communication, and widespread reach. In such scenarios, individuals may struggle to balance personal integrity, loyalty, justice, compassion, individual rights, and community welfare, often under the pressure of real-time decision-making and the potential for significant social impact. Crowder and Turvey (2013) list these ethical dilemmas as follows in table 3.1. The example scenarios can be discussed with kids and teenagers to better understand their judgments in each case.

PROMOTING BENEVOLENT INTERACTIONS IN ONLINE GAMES: SOCIAL EXCHANGE THEORY

In a study, Jang et al. (2016) explored the motivation behind posting benevolent comments online to counter cyberbullying through the lens of Social Exchange Theory (SET). SET helps us understand social behavior and social structures through the analysis of exchanges between individuals and groups. This theory, developed by notable scholars such as Homans (1961), Blau (1964), and Emerson (1962), is rooted in utilitarianism and behaviorism (Cook & Rice, 2003). SET encompasses several key principles:

- **Exchange of Activities:** Social exchange involves the transfer of tangible or intangible activities that carry rewards or costs between at least two individuals.
- **Reinforcement Principles:** Behavior is influenced by rewards and punishments, reflecting principles from behaviorism.
- **Dyadic and Network Exchanges:** Social exchanges can occur in dyadic (two-person) relationships or within larger social networks, thus influencing broader social structures.
- **Power and Dependence:** Power in social exchanges is a function of the dependence of one actor on another for valued resources. Power is relational and can affect social structures.
- **Emergent Properties:** Social exchanges can create emergent properties, such as social structures and institutions, which subsequently influence future exchanges.

In understanding SET, emotions and power are two crucial concepts. Positive emotions, such as satisfaction and trust, can strengthen social bonds and commitment, while negative emotions, like anger and resentment, can weaken them. Power imbalances occur when one party controls more valued resources than another, leading to dependency.

SET provides a useful framework for understanding social interactions, emotional responses, and power dynamics in online gaming and cyberbullying. Social exchanges in gaming, such as cooperation, competition, and resource sharing, are driven by perceived benefits (e.g., in-game rewards, social status) and costs (e.g., time, effort). The study by Jang et al. (2016) suggests that promoting benevolent behaviors, like supportive comments, can create a positive social norm within gaming communities. However, the same power dynamics and emotional exchanges that facilitate positive interactions can also lead to cyberbullying, as players with more power or higher status may exploit these dynamics to bully others. Encouraging benevolent comments among gamers can foster a supportive culture that counters the negative impact of cyberbullying behaviors.

To achieve this, several design approaches are essential. Implementing a gamified reward system where players earn points, badges, or in-game perks for posting supportive comments can foster a culture of positivity. Additionally, utilizing AI-powered moderation tools to monitor chat, highlight positive interactions, and automatically flag or remove harmful comments ensures that benevolent behavior is recognized and promoted in real time. Finally, incorporating educational modules within the game that teach players about the impact of their online behavior, emphasizing empathy, respect, and the benefits of positive communication, can further encourage a more supportive gaming community.

"REFLECT AND REFRAME" FOR ADULTS

1. What do you enjoy most about playing group games online?
2. Have you ever been angry during an online game? How did you handle it, and how did it affect your interactions with other players?
3. Think about a time when you or a friend experienced trash-talking in an online game. When do you think this behavior crosses the line into cyberbullying?
4. Have you noticed any differences in how players from different cultures behave in online games? How do these cultural differences shape the way cyberbullying is perceived and managed in various gaming communities?
5. What are some practical steps you can take to create a safer and more supportive environment in your online gaming experiences?

How can in-game tools and community guidelines help address cyberbullying?
6. How can understanding netiquette help reduce instances of cyberbullying in online games? Can you name five netiquette rules that you think are important to follow and promote?
7. Can you recall a time when you encountered acronyms or slang in online gaming chats that you didn't understand? How did it make you feel, and what could you do to stay informed about these terms and their meanings?

"REFLECT AND REFRAME" FOR KIDS

1. What do you like about playing games with friends online?
2. Have you ever felt mad during an online game? What did you do, and how did it change how you played with others?
3. Has anyone ever said mean things during a game? When does it become bullying?
4. Do people from different places act differently in games? How does this affect bullying?

5. What can you do to make online games safer and nicer? How can game rules help?
6. How can being nice online help stop bullying? Can you name five good manners to follow in games?
7. Have you ever seen words in game chats that you didn't understand? How did it make you feel, and how can you learn what they mean?

REFERENCES

AlJaffer, M., Alshehri, K., Almutairi, M., Aljumaiah, A., Alfraiji, A., Hakami, M., & Irfan, T. (2021). Cyberbullying among young Saudi online gamers and its relation to depression. *Journal of Nature and Science of Medicine, 4*(2), 142–147.

Blau, P. M. (1964). *Exchange and power in social life.* New York: Wiley.

CEOP Education. (2024). In-game chat: What parents and carers need to know. https://www.ceopeducation.co.uk/parents/articles/in-game-chat/#:~:text=Some%20people%20online%20genuinely%20just,don't%20want%20to%20do

Cook, K. S., & Rice, E. (2003). Social exchange theory. In J. Delamater (Ed.), *Handbook of social psychology* (pp. 53–76). Kluwer Academic/Plenum Publishers.

Crowder, S., & Turvey, B. E. (Eds.). (2013). Ethics in the criminal justice professions. In *Ethical justice: Applied issues for criminal justice students and professionals*, 1st ed. Academic Press. https://doi.org/10.1016/B978-0-12-404597-2.00001-2

Emerson, R. (1962). Power-dependence relations. *American Sociological Review, 27*, 31–41.

Homans, G. C. (1961). *Social behavior and its elementary forms.* New York: Harcourt, Brace and World. https://www.washingtonpost.com/technology/2019/02/26/racism-misogynydeath-threats-why-cant-booming-video-game-industry-curb-toxicity/

Jang, Y. J., Kim, H. W., & Jung, Y. (2016). A mixed methods approach to the posting of benevolent comments online. *International Journal of Information Management, 36*(3), 414–424.

Kaye, L. S., Hellsten, L., McIntyre, L. J., & Hendry, B. P. (2022). 'There's a fine line between trash-talking and cyberbullying': A qualitative exploration of youth perspectives of online gaming culture. *International Review of Sociology, 32*(3), 426–442. https://doi.org/10.1080/03906701.2022.2133407

Kowert, R. (2020). Dark participation in games. *Frontiers in Psychology, 11*, 29–69. https://doi.org/10.3389/fpsyg.2020.598947

Kwak, H., Blackburn, J., & Han, S. (2015). Exploring cyberbullying and other toxic behavior in team competition online games. *Proceedings of the 33rd annual ACM conference on human factors in computing systems.* New York, NY, USA. https://doi.org/10.1145/2702123.2702529

Lam, L. T., Cheng, Z., & Liu, X. (2013). Violent online games exposure and cyberbullying/victimization among adolescents. *Cyberpsychology, Behavior, and Social Networking, 16*(3), 159–165.

Maldonado, M. (2016, May 17). Frustration with video games leads to aggressive behavior. *PsychCentral.* https://psychcentral.com/lib/frustration-withvideo-games -leads-to-aggressive-behavior#1

McInroy, L. B., & Mishna, F. (2017). Cyberbullying on online gaming platforms for children and youth. *Child and Adolescent Social Work Journal, 34*, 597–607.

Morin, A. (2022). The secret language of teens: 116 text and social media acronyms. https://www.verywellfamily.com/the-secret-language-of-teens-100-social-media -acronyms-2609651

Park, S., Na, E. Y., & Kim, E. M. (2014). The relationship between online activities, netiquette and cyberbullying. *Children and Youth Services Review, 42*, 74–81.

Scott, J., & Porter-Armstrong, A. P. (2013). Impact of multiplayer online role-playing games upon the psychosocial well-being of adolescents and young adults: Reviewing the evidence. *Psychiatry Journal, 2013*, 464685. https://doi.org/10.1155/2013 /464685

Smith, N. (2019, February 26). Racism, misogyny, death threats: Why can't the booming video-game industry curb toxicity? *The Washington Post.*

Yang, S. C. (2012). Paths to bullying in online gaming: The effects of gender, preference for playing violent games, hostility, and aggressive behavior on bullying. *Journal of Educational Computing Research, 47*(3), 235–249.

Chapter 4

The Psychology of Online Trolling

LEARNING OBJECTIVES

Upon completion of this chapter, you will be able to:

1. Analyze the psychological and social factors contributing to trolling behavior among teens.
2. Evaluate the impact of different forms of online harassment, such as trolling, doxing, and message bombing, on individuals and communities.
3. Discuss effective strategies for managing and mitigating the effects of online trolling.
4. Examine the role of personality traits and environmental factors in influencing online trolling behavior.

In April 2024, Indian school exam topper Prachi Nigam, who scored 98.5 percent on her board exams, faced online trolling due to her facial hair when her photo was posted on social media. Despite the hurtful comments, Prachi responded with resilience, stating, "However God has made me, I am okay with it," and continued to focus on her studies. Her experience highlights the persistent issue of trolling among teens, where achievements are overshadowed by superficial judgments (News Source).

Reflecting on this news, it's clear that the psychology of trolling can be deeply rooted in societal norms and expectations, as well as factors such as anonymity, power dynamics, underlying psychological issues, and group mentality. Trolls can target not only individuals' physical appearances but also personal beliefs, intellectual abilities, interests and hobbies, social status, and family and relationships. Prachi's response, one of ignoring the trolls and maintaining self-acceptance, stands as one of the most effective strategies to deal with online harassment.

Trolling is one of the many forms of online harassment, sharing common ground with other malicious activities such as message bombing, doxxing, and revenge porn. These types of harassment all contribute to creating a hostile online environment and can have severe real-world consequences. Trolling involves making negative or hurtful comments intended to upset, humiliate, or discredit someone. Similarly, message bombing entails sending an excessive number of texts, chats, instant messages, or emails to block access to the recipient's account, often with the help of bots. Doxxing involves sharing someone's personal information online, such as their phone number or home address, which can facilitate identity theft or lead to harassment both online and offline. Revenge porn, another severe form of harassment, involves sharing sexually explicit photographs or videos of an individual without their consent. There is a large volume of literature that studies the psychology of trolling.

Online trolling is a multifaceted concept that involves various behaviors aimed at provoking and antagonizing others. According to Herring, Job-Sluder, Scheckler, and Barab (2002), trolling is defined as "luring others into often pointless and time-consuming discussions" (p. 373). Hardaker (2013) further explains that trolls draw other users or communities into distracting and irrelevant discussions, specifically targeting inexperienced or naive users with incorrect or inappropriate messages. Shachaf and Hara (2010) note that trolls engage in intentionally repetitive and harmful actions, often violating community policies out of boredom, attention seeking, and the pursuit of entertainment, which damages the community, its content, and its members. Thus, it appears that trolling is essentially about abusing others for personal enjoyment in the online sphere (Bishop, 2014).

PHOTOBOMBING AND ZOOMBOMBING

You might be familiar with the terms photobombing and Zoombombing. Photobomb trolling involves intentionally inserting oneself into the background of a photo being taken by others, often striking a humorous or exaggerated pose to disrupt the intended scene. Photobombers aim to elicit laughter and amusement from both the subjects of the photo and those who view the final image.

This type of trolling satirizes the oft-posed and contrived nature of photographs, especially those taken at popular tourist destinations or during significant events. Similarly, Zoombombing involves intruding into a Zoom video conference call uninvited, often to display inappropriate content or disrupt the meeting. Just as photobombing disrupts the original intent of a photo, internet trolls can alter the focus of online posts by spreading false information or personally attacking individuals to provoke emotional reactions and create chaos.

Unlike the playful intent behind photobombing, malicious trolling is driven by a desire to upset others, often for the troll's personal amusement or to undermine community cohesion. This harmful behavior highlights the darker side of trolling, where the objective shifts from shared enjoyment to deliberate antagonism and abuse (see figure 4.1).

PERSONALITY TRAITS AND ENVIRONMENTAL FACTORS CONTRIBUTING TO TROLLING

Scholars from various disciplines examined the potential reasons and motivations to be a troll in different contexts. For example, in the paper "Trolls Just Want to Have Fun," Buckels, Trapnell, and Paulhus (2014) explored the personality traits of internet trolls through two studies with a total of 1,215 participants in the United States and Canada contexts. Using personality inventories and surveys on internet commenting styles, the researchers found

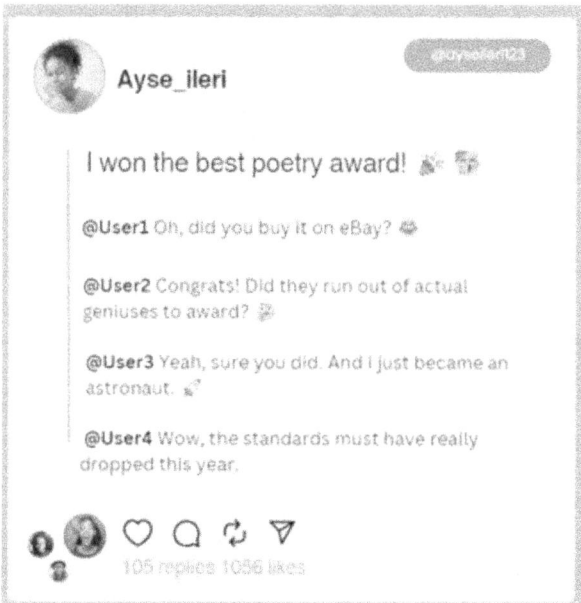

Figure 4.1 An Example of Twitter (X) Trolling. *Source*: Author generated using Canva.com.

strong positive associations between trolling behaviors and the Dark Tetrad of personality traits: sadism, narcissism, psychopathy, and Machiavellianism. Sadism showed the strongest correlation, indicating that trolls derive pleasure specifically from causing distress to others.

These findings suggest that internet trolling is primarily an expression of everyday sadism, where individuals engage in antisocial behavior online for personal enjoyment. It is important to highlight that the enjoyment of other online activities, such as chatting and debating, was found to be unrelated to sadism. Furthermore, narcissism was negatively related to trolling enjoyment, suggesting that trolls are less likely to be narcissistic. Finally, Buckels et al. (2014) identified a strong positive relation between online commenting frequency and trolling enjoyment.

Howard and colleagues (2019) also found how gender and a lack of empathy contribute to malicious online activities. Males were found to be significantly more likely to engage in trolling, and trolls typically demonstrate reduced empathy, which aligns with their disruptive and harmful behavior.

In another study, Seigfried-Spellar and Lankford (2018) studied personality traits and online sharing behaviors and found that different personality traits and environmental factors influence how people post on an anonymous social media platform, Yik Yak. This pseudonymous app enables users to create and view discussion threads within a five-mile radius. The authors' study surveyed 173 undergraduate students at a large Southern University and found that trolls, posters, lurkers, and confessors exhibit distinct personality profiles and online behaviors.

Trolls scored significantly higher on psychopathy, had a higher acceptability of prejudiced comments, and lower agreeableness, aligning with their tendency to post offensive comments for amusement. Confessors, who often share personal information anonymously, showed higher levels of neuroticism, Machiavellianism, and feelings of reduced accountability online, but lower social moral values. Lurkers, who read but do not post, scored higher on conscientiousness and lower on Machiavellianism, indicating a more observant and less manipulative nature.

Loneliness is also found as another predictor of trolling behavior. According to Keita Masui (2019), higher levels of loneliness amplified the tendency to engage in trolling. These findings highlight that internet trolling is not only influenced by personality traits but also exacerbated by feelings of loneliness, suggesting a complex interaction between psychological factors and online behavior.

Another study also examined the trolling behaviors on Yik Yak to see the impacts of territorial communication norms and community composition on trolling behaviors (Fichman & Peters, 2019). As we earlier discussed, Yik Yak is a geolocation-based program that allows anonymous discussion within a five-mile radius. The findings indicated that trolling, characterized by vulgar language and insults, increased during local events such as sporting weekends when the community size grew due to visitors. Conversely, trolling behaviors decreased during more solemn events like graduation weekends. The study also found that community reactions to trolling were often humorous or lighthearted. The anonymity feature of Yik Yak facilitated trolling by reducing accountability, while geolocation fostered a sense of community that influenced deviant behaviors. These findings offer important insights regarding the complex interplay between communication platform features, community norms, and external events in shaping online trolling behaviors. The next section discusses trolling tactics as studied and discussed by the published literature.

SUCCESSFUL TROLLING TACTICS

Understanding successful trolling tactics can help online communities better identify and manage trolling behaviors.

For instance, in a study aimed at understanding how trolling behaviors are managed within a feminist online discussion forum, Herring et al. (2002) explored the strategies used by trolls to disrupt online communities and the responses of the community to such disruptions. The research questions focused on how trolls successfully disrupt online feminist forums, what strategies feminist online communities use to manage trolling, and how effective these strategies are in maintaining a safe and supportive online environment. The study was set in the context of a feminist web-based discussion forum with over 4,000 members. This forum, which serves as a space for dialogue on feminist issues, was significantly disrupted over almost two months by a troll named Kent.

Kent's successful trolling strategies included presenting themselves as a sincere debaters, using flame bait, and provoking futile arguments. Flame bait refers to inflammatory or provocative comments designed to elicit an emotional response and ignite heated debates, often causing disruption and diverting the conversation from its original topic. Provoking futile arguments, on the other hand, involves initiating debates on controversial or sensitive issues where no resolution is likely, thereby exhausting the community members' patience and resources.

In a similar vein, Fishman and Dainas (2019) identified various tactics used by trolls on Tumblr to provoke outrage. These tactics include attacking someone's character, starting conflicts, showing extreme emotions, using strong emotional words, pushing extreme viewpoints, using insulting language, exaggerating things to misrepresent them, mocking people, calling them names, using obscene language, making slippery slope arguments, and engaging in verbal fights. Each tactic is designed to provoke and disrupt online communities. For example, pushing extreme viewpoints and exaggerating things to misrepresent them were frequently employed to inflame tensions and provoke strong reactions. These tactics help trolls gain attention and create chaos within the community, often using deceptive and inflammatory language to achieve their goals.

EFFECTIVE STRATEGIES FOR DEALING WITH TROLLING

As educators, it is crucial to understand the social psychology behind trolling to predict and limit its harmful effects. What motivates trolls to engage in trolling? According to Communication Scientist Susan Herring and her collaborators (2002), a common factor in the observed trolling incidents is that trolls seem to enjoy the attention they receive, even, and possibly more so, when it is consistently negative.

Educating users about the tactics of trolls and the patterns they follow can also prevent their effects, similar to warning about phone pranks or sales scams. Internet users must be trained about the signs of trolling, such as unbelievable claims or cross-posted messages, and advised on how to respond.

Hardaker (2015, p. 223) identifies seven types of responses to trolls, derived from a discourse analysis of online trolling instances:

1. Responding sincerely to the troll.
2. Ignoring the trolling attempt, either openly or subtly.
3. Revealing the troll's actions to the group.
4. Challenging the troll, either directly or indirectly.
5. Critiquing and commenting on the troll's effectiveness or quality.
6. Mocking or parodying the trolling attempt.
7. Counter-trolling by mirroring the troll's behavior.

Using humor, fighting back with facts and statistics, and correcting them are among the strategies recommended at the individual level (Rampton, 2015).

"REFLECT AND REFRAME" FOR ADULTS

1. Have you ever witnessed or been the target of a troll attack? How did it unfold, and what impact did it have on you or the community involved?
2. How do societal norms and expectations influence the behavior of online trolls, and in what ways might this shape your perception of trolling?
3. How has the anonymity of the internet affected your experiences with online interactions, and what role do power dynamics play in the prevalence of trolling?
4. What psychological traits are commonly associated with trolls, and how have you recognized these behaviors in your own online interactions?
5. In what ways can online communities effectively identify and manage trolling behaviors to create a more supportive environment, and how have you seen this implemented?

"REFLECT AND REFRAME" FOR KIDS

1. Have you ever seen someone being mean online? What happened, and how did it make you feel?
2. Do you think people act differently online because of rules? How does it change what you think about them?
3. How does hiding who you are change how people talk online? How do people use power to be mean online?
4. What kinds of people are often mean online? How have you seen these people act in your own online games?
5. How can online groups find and stop mean behaviors to make things nicer for everyone?

REFERENCES

Bishop, J. (2014). Representations of "trolls" in mass media communication: A review of media-texts and moral panics relating to "Internet trolling." *International Journal of Web Based Communities*, *10*(1), 7–24. https://doi.org/10.1504/IJWBC .2014.058384

Buckels, E. E., Trapnell, P. D., & Paulhus, D. L. (2014). Trolls just want to have fun. *Personality and Individual Differences*, *67*, 97–102.

CoPilot. (2024, June 3). An image generated by microsoft copilot. The following prompt was used: "Create a scene where a family is taking a fun photo in Istanbul, and someone in the background is making a weird pose."

Fichman, P., & Dainas, A. (2018). Graphicons and tactics in satirical trolling on Tumblr.com. *International Journal of Communication, 13*, 4261–4286.

Fichman, P., & Peters, E. (2019). The impacts of territorial communication norms and composition on online trolling. *International Journal of Communication, 13*, 20.

Hardaker, C. (2013). "Uh . . . not to be nitpicky, but . . . the past tense of drag is dragged, not drug": An overview of trolling strategies. *Journal of Language Aggression and Conflict, 1*(1), 58–86.

Hardaker, C. (2015). 'I refuse to respond to this obvious troll': An overview of responses to (perceived) trolling. *Corpora, 10*(2), 201–229.

Herring, S., Job-Sluder, K., Scheckler, R., & Barab, S. (2002). Searching for safety online: Managing "Trolling" in a feminist forum. *The Information Society, 18*, 371–384.

Howard, K., Zolnierek, K. H., Critz, K., Dailey, S., & Ceballos, N. (2019). An examination of psychosocial factors associated with malicious online trolling behaviors. *Personality and Individual Differences, 149*, 309–314.

Masui, K. (2019). Loneliness moderates the relationship between Dark Tetrad personality traits and internet trolling. *Personality and Individual Differences, 150*, 109475.

Rampton, J. (2015, April 9). 10 tips to dealing with trolls. *Forbes*. Retrieved from http://www.forbes.com/sites/johnrampton/2015/04/09/10-tips-to-dealing-with-trolls/

Seigfried-Spellar, K. C., & Lankford, C. M. (2018). Personality and online environment factors differ for posters, trolls, lurkers, and confessors on Yik Yak. *Personality and Individual Differences, 124*, 54–56.

Shachaf, P., & Hara, N. (2010). Beyond vandalism: Wikipedia trolls. *Journal of Information Science, 36*(3), 357–370.

Chapter 5

Harmful Social Media Trends

LEARNING OBJECTIVES

Upon completion of this chapter, you will be able to:

1. Identify and analyze the impact of harmful social media trends on mental and physical health.
2. Evaluate the influence of social media on cultural norms and personal behaviors among adolescents.
3. Discuss strategies for managing and mitigating the negative effects of viral social media challenges.
4. Examine the role of parental guidance and community support in preventing the spread of dangerous online activities.

INTRODUCTION

In recent years, platforms such as TikTok, Instagram, YouTube, and Twitter have become integral parts of daily life, reshaping cultural norms and personal behaviors, including how individuals think, interact, communicate, live their social lives, and even fall in love (Chukwuere & Chukwuere, 2017). For example, trends that dramatize or fabricate scenarios of infidelity or excessively romanticized portrayals of relationships can set unrealistic expectations, causing individuals to feel inadequate if their relationships do not match these idealized standards (Lariat, 2024). This chapter explores various viral social media trends such as bed rotting, skincare routines, choking yourself until you pass out, and drinking challenges that can cause significant mental and physical harm.

WHAT IS BED ROTTING?

The phenomenon of "bed rotting" is a trending topic on social media platforms, particularly on TikTok, where it has garnered significant attention among Gen Z, who were born between 1997 and 2012 (Dimock, 2019). Bed rotting involves staying in bed for extended periods, often the entire day, engaging in activities like watching videos, scrolling through social media, or sleeping.

Advocates of bed rotting argue that it serves as a form of self-care, helping to manage stress and anxiety by rejecting the pressures of productivity culture.

Despite its popularity, the bed rotting trend has faced criticism from health professionals since extended periods of inactivity can lead to physical health issues, such as weight gain and muscle atrophy, as well as mental health concerns like increased feelings of depression and anxiety (Foreback, 2023). To decrease these risks, alternative strategies for managing stress and improving mental health are recommended, such as ensuring quality sleep at night, engaging in daily exercise, maintaining a healthy diet, and practicing mindfulness activities like meditation, journaling, or yoga (Kubota, 2023).

While the bed rotting trend offers a temporary escape and a form of empowerment against societal pressures, it is important to approach it with caution and moderation. Parents and guardians should be particularly vigilant about repeated bed rotting behaviors accompanied by digital entertainment in children, as it can hinder their social and emotional development and lead to physical health issues.

QUALITATIVE CONTENT ANALYSIS OF REDDIT COMMENTS ON "BED ROTTING" TREND

A thematic analysis of the first 200 Reddit comments (https://www.reddit .com/r/Adulting/comments/174rikc/thoughts_on_the_bed_rotting_trend/) on the "bed rotting" trend revealed five main key themes, highlighting diverse opinions and experiences related to this phenomenon. These themes include the need for rest and recuperation, mental health perspectives, societal views on productivity, criticisms of the trend, and the importance of moderation.

Many users identified the need for rest and recuperation, emphasizing it as essential in a society that undervalues rest, with comments like, "Rest is fantastic. However, you want to do that is perfectly fine." Mental health perspectives varied, with some seeing "bed rotting" as beneficial, while others viewed it as a symptom of deeper issues: "I struggle with some mental health things. So this doesn't universally apply. However, at some point, I just gave

Table 5.1 Bed Rotting Themes and Frequencies

Theme	Frequency	Representative Example
Need for Rest and Recuperation	45	"It's not 'rotting,' it's restorative. The human equivalent of defragging your computer and clearing the caches."
Mental Health Perspectives	50	"Sometimes it's good to just 'give up' for a moment or a while to recuperate. Some people isolate for more than 1 or so years, it all depends on a person."
Societal Views on Productivity	40	"It's kind of like a rejection of productivity culture by doing nothing and taking the time to rest."
Criticisms of the Trend	35	"If I spend much time lying awake in bed, my body forgets how to fall asleep in it when I need to."
Importance of Moderation	30	"Most forms of rest are great when used in moderation. Staying in your bed all day is objectively, absolutely fine."

myself permission to have 'a bad day'." Societal views on productivity were critical, with users seeing the trend as a rebellion against constant productivity demands: "It's kind of like a rejection of productivity culture by doing nothing and taking the time to rest." Criticisms of the trend highlighted potential negative health implications and the problematic name: "The only thing I have against 'bed rot' is the name, it's not. We are all exhausted." Lastly, the importance of moderation was emphasized, warning against excessive rest: "Most forms of rest are great when used in moderation. Staying in your bed all day is objectively, absolutely fine." (See table 5.1.)

SKIN CARE TRENDS: CLEAN GIRL AESTHETIC

Social media significantly influences how young people perceive beauty, skincare, and self-care too (Portela, 2023). Dr. Dustin Portela (2023) highlights the dual-edged impact of TikTok on skincare awareness. While the platform has positively educated many about good skincare practices and high-quality products, it has also propagated harmful DIY skincare trends and the use of unregulated products like the hyaluron pen and melanotan. These trends often result in skin damage, allergic reactions, and other health risks due to the misuse of ingredients and lack of proper clinical testing. The rise of "skinfluencers" without credentials exacerbates these issues by spreading misinformation. Dr. Portela emphasizes the need for dermatologists to actively educate the public to counteract these harmful trends.

DIY skincare routines and the "clean girl" aesthetic are among these harmful trends that often lead to the unregulated use of multiple skincare products without proper guidance, resulting in adverse skin reactions. The "clean girl" aesthetic, promoting minimalistic yet flawless routines, exacerbates societal pressures on appearance, contributing to anxiety and self-esteem issues among adolescents.

In empirical research, Galamgam and Jia (2021) explored how teenagers and young adults engage with information about acne treatment, particularly isotretinoin, on TikTok. Analysis of the top fifty videos on this trend, which accumulated over 18 million likes and 137 thousand comments, revealed that most videos focused on before-and-after improvements in acne severity. Comments often discussed side effects and personal anecdotes. The findings suggest that TikTok serves as a significant platform for dermatological education, though it may skew perceptions of isotretinoin's efficacy and side effects. This mirrors the current skincare trends among young teenagers, where social media heavily influences their use of skincare products, sometimes leading to inappropriate or excessive usage, similar to young girls' fascination with advanced skincare products like anti-aging creams and glycolic acid peels.

Another particularly concerning trend is "Sephora Kids," where young children engage in beauty routines aimed at adults (Dauber, 2024). This trend is often fueled by influencer marketing and social media platforms showcasing young children using high-end beauty products. The trend highlights the significant influence of social media on younger audiences, often pushing them toward products they do not need and promoting an unhealthy focus on appearance and consumption (Dauber, 2024).

10-YEAR-OLDS ARE TAKING OVER SEPHORA: YOUTUBE VIDEO COMMENT ANALYSIS

To better understand public reactions to the Sephora Kids concept, I examined user comments on a YouTube video titled "10-Year-Olds Are Taking Over Sephora." The video highlights a recent trend where preteens are reportedly causing chaos in Sephora stores. These young girls, moving beyond traditional toys, are now engaging with high-end makeup brands, particularly causing distress among Sephora employees and customers. The main complaints involve these children trashing makeup displays, mixing testers, and creating messes. Employees recount incidents of theft, disrespectful behavior, and inappropriate use of products. The video also raises concerns about the financial burden on parents and the potential skin damage to young girls using products like anti-aging creams. Ultimately, the video critiques both the trend and the name "Sephora Kids."

This video was selected since it received 3.2 million views and 12,925 comments. The high number of comments provided a great opportunity to better understand the reaction of the public to the Sephora Kids phenomenon.

The comments were extracted using software called Export Comments (https://exportcomments.com/). Next, an open coding strategy was implemented, where each comment was read, and memos were written for each one. Repeated themes were noted and documented, allowing emerging themes to develop inductively. In the second phase, the comments were reread, and memos were written again, with a focus on refining and expanding themes, as well as incorporating focused coding to analyze perspectives on skincare and young teenagers. The final phase involved reviewing and combining similar themes, providing clear definitions for each.

The content analysis findings revealed several key themes: (1) use of makeup as an art form and self-expression, (2) parental influence on skincare routines, (3) peer pressure, (4) calls for better regulation and supervision, and (5) simplicity of past skincare routines.

A frequently recurring theme is the use of makeup as an art form and a means of self-expression. For instance, one user mentions, "I am 13 and I wear makeup sometimes to try to bring some of the characters from stories to life," highlighting how makeup is used creatively rather than just for beauty enhancement. Similarly, another comment states, "I like to play around with makeup but as an art form. I love expressing myself via makeup."

Parental influence on skincare routines is another significant theme. Some users have learned skincare habits from their parents, emphasizing the importance of early education. One user shares, "From an early age, I was taught to take good care of my skin. I started doing my routine at 13." However, there are also criticisms of parents who allow their children to misuse makeup and skincare products. Comments such as, "These parents are horrible, they're letting their kids get makeup they don't need, they're letting their kids trash the public," reflect the frustration with the lack of parental control and guidance.

Next, peer influence was a prominent theme, with many young users mimicking trends they see online. This often leads to inappropriate behaviors, as highlighted by the comment, "These kids are allowed onto social media along with the rest of us, and what do kids like to do? Imitate the older 'cooler' kids to fit in." The influence of social media also raises concerns about the use of unsuitable products, with one user noting, "I wish the 'anti-aging skincare' the children were getting obsessed with was sunscreen . . . hearing about children using retinol and chemical peels makes me so nervous."

There are also calls for better regulation and supervision in stores like Sephora to prevent such issues. For instance, one commentor suggests,

"Maybe Sephora should make a few aisles of stuff for the teens so they don't accidentally mess their skin up." This sentiment is echoed in other comments advocating for age restrictions, such as, "Okay it's time they make these stores 18+."

Additionally, many users reflect on the simplicity of past skincare routines compared to the complex routines of today's preteens. Comments like, "When I was their age, my skincare was water only, and I'm only a few years older than them," and "My skincare to this day contains tap water," emphasize the drastic changes in skincare practices over time.

DANGEROUS ONLINE ACTIVITIES AND CHALLENGES

Choking Challenge and Black Out Rage Gallon (BORG) are among the social media challenges tragically resulting in the deaths of children since the 2000s. The Choking/Blackout Challenge, in particular, compels participants to choke themselves to the point of unconsciousness, seeking a brief euphoric state induced by oxygen deprivation (Chan, 2018). In a lawsuit, the grieving parents of two preteen girls, aged eight and nine, who succumbed to this challenge, accused TikTok of fostering addictive algorithms that led to their untimely deaths (Yang, 2022).

Most recently, this choking challenge led to two students passing out in South Orange, New Jersey. One student had to be hospitalized due to difficulty breathing after regaining consciousness, and the other was treated by the school nursing staff (Felbin et al., 2024). The CDC has released a list of indicators that might suggest someone is attempting the choking challenge, which include bloodshot eyes, marks on the neck, severe headaches, and feeling disoriented after spending time alone (Felbin et al., 2024). Raising awareness of these signs among parents, health care providers, and educators is crucial to prevent further incidents.

BORG, a dangerous drinking trend popularized on TikTok, involves consuming large quantities of alcohol mixed with water, caffeine, vitamins, artificial sweeteners, food dyes, and cannabis (Watson, 2024).

The article titled "Black Out Rage Gallon (aka borg): An Investigation of a Risky Drinking Trend on TikTok" by Mandzufas and colleagues (2024) conducted a content analysis of 103 TikTok videos associated with the #borg hashtag, noting that alcohol was visible in three-quarters of the videos and consumed in one-third. While 25 percent of the videos promoted alleged benefits of borg consumption, such as controlling alcohol intake and preventing drink spiking, only 9 percent included warnings about potential harms. The study highlighted the rapid spread and high engagement of these videos, with over 60 percent posted within ten weeks and garnering nearly seven million likes.

The authors summarized their major findings as follows:

- High Visibility and Consumption: Alcohol was prominently visible in most videos, and rapid or excessive consumption was often depicted.
- Perceived Benefits: Some videos claimed benefits of borg consumption, like harm minimization and hydration, but these were misleading.
- Lack of Warnings: Few videos warned about the dangers of BORG consumption, despite the significant health risks.

The study also emphasizes the necessity for public health professionals to actively counteract such harmful trends on social media by posting educational content that highlights the risks associated with risky drinking behaviors.

WHAT TO DO WHEN YOU SEE AN ONLINE CHALLENGE?

TikTok advises users to follow a four-step process: STOP, THINK, DECIDE, and ACT (https://www.tiktok.com/safety/en/reporting). This involves pausing to consider the safety, respectfulness, and authenticity of the challenge. Users should critically assess whether the challenge could cause harm, whether it respects others, and if it is a legitimate activity or a hoax. If the challenge is deemed risky or harmful, users are encouraged not to participate and to report it using the in-app reporting tools.

For parents, guardians, and educators, TikTok emphasizes the importance of discussing online challenges with teens, who may lack the experience to assess risks effectively. The guidelines suggest engaging in open conversations to help teens identify potential dangers, consider the consequences, and make safe choices. The goal is to balance awareness of risks with the understanding that some challenges can offer positive experiences, like fostering creativity or social connections, while ensuring that safety remains a priority.

THOUGHT-PROVOKING QUESTIONS BEFORE POSTING SOMETHING ON SOCIAL MEDIA

The below rubric is designed to help adolescents critically evaluate their social media posts before sharing them online. By considering aspects such as self-awareness, purpose and appropriateness, relationship building and communication, and cultural understanding, this tool encourages thoughtful and responsible online behavior. (See table 5.2.)

Table 5.2 Examples of Self-Reflective Questions to Consider Before Posting Online

Theme	Questions to Consider	Rating (1–5) ★ ★ ★ ★ ★
Self-awareness	• Have I reflected on my social media habits, and does this post align with healthy use? • Have I considered the potential risks and consequences of participating in or promoting a social media challenge? • Am I aware of the motivations behind this challenge, and do they align with my values? • Does this challenge promote positive behavior, or could it be harmful to myself or others?	
Purpose and appropriateness	• What is my objective in posting this content? • Is social media the best platform for this post? • Would I be comfortable with my post being shared widely or viewed by unintended audiences? • Could my post harm someone or impact their ability to work?	
Relationship building and communication	• Does my post help build positive relationships? • Could my post blur the lines between reality and fantasy? • Does my post support healthy and respectful online communication?	
Cultural understanding	• Does my post share cultural knowledge or understanding? • Could my post be seen as perpetuating stereotypes or negative views?	

Scoring Guide:

1. **Strongly Disagree:** Does not meet the criteria at all.
2. **Disagree:** Meets the criteria somewhat.
3. **Neutral:** Meets the criteria moderately.
4. **Agree:** Meets the criteria well.
5. **Strongly Agree:** Meets the criteria exceptionally well.

"REFLECT AND REFRAME" FOR ADULTS

1. Reflect on a time when you felt pressured to conform to a social media trend. How did you handle it, and what did you learn from the experience?
2. How do you think trends like "bed rotting" challenge societal expectations of productivity and self-care?
3. What strategies can you use to critically assess the safety and authenticity of a social media challenge before participating?
4. How can parents and guardians effectively guide teenagers about the pressures and influences of social media?

"REFLECT AND REFRAME" FOR KIDS

1. Have you ever felt like you had to do something because everyone else was doing it online, like a dance or a challenge? What did you do, and what did you learn?
2. How do you think staying in bed all day (like "bed rotting") changes what people think about being busy and taking care of yourself?
3. How can you and your parents check if an online challenge is safe before trying it?
4. How can you and your parents talk about the pressures of using social media?

REFERENCES

Berwick, C. (2024). Social media performance in school: Youth practice of humor and resistance through TikTok trends. *E-Learning and Digital Media*, 0(0). https://doi.org/10.1177/20427530241241766

Brophy, A. (2022, August 18). A gen zer's view of the future of social media and the metaverse. *PR Daily*. Retrieved from www.prdaily.com/a-gen-zers-view-of-the-future-of-social-media-and-the-metaverse/

Chan, M. (2018, March 12). Kids are playing the 'choking game' to get high. Instead, they're dying. *TIME*. Retrieved from https://time.com/5189584/choking-game-pass-out-challenge/

Chukwuere, J. E., & Chukwuere, P. C. (2017). The impact of social media on social lifestyle: A case study of university female students. *Gender & Behavior*, *15*(4), 9966–9981.

Dauber, R. (2024, April 4). Sephora Kids point to the overconsumption of TikTok trends. *The Student Newspaper of Washington College*.

Dimock, M. (2019). Defining generations: Where millennials end and generation Z begins. Retrieved from https://www.pewresearch.org/short-reads/2019/01/17/where-millennials-end-and-generation-z-begins/

Felbin, S., Talbert, S., & Aloian, A. (2024, April 17). The 'blackout challenge' has resurfaced on Tiktok, and it's still just as dangerous as it was 17 years ago. *Women's Health*. Retrieved from https://www.womenshealthmag.com/health/a38603617/blackout-challenge-tiktok-2021/

Galamgam, J., & Jia, J. L. (2021). "Accutane check": Insights into youth sentiment toward isotretinoin from a TikTok trend. *Pediatric Dermatology*, *38*(4), 980–981.

Kubota, S. (2023). What is bed rotting, and is it good for you? What to know about the Gen Z trend. Retrieved from https://www.today.com/health/news/bed-rotting-rcna108074

Lariat, B. (2024). Toxic social media trends take toll on relationships. Retrieved from https://baylorlariat.com/2024/02/06/toxic-social-media-trends-take-toll-on-relationships/

Mandzufas, J., Lim, N., McPhie, S., Martin, C., Johnston, R. S., Lombardi, K., & Trapp, G. S. (2024). 'Black Out Rage Gallon' (aka borg): An investigation of a risky drinking trend on TikTok. *Health Promotion Journal of Australia*.

Portela, D. (2023, June 26). Harmful social media skin care trends: Viral doesn't mean safe. *Dermatology Times*, *44*(6). Retrieved from https://www.dermatologytimes.com/view/harmful-social-media-skin-care-trends-viral-doesn-t-mean-safe

Watson, S. (2024, June 5). What is a BORG? *WebMD*. Retrieved from https://www.webmd.com/mental-health/addiction/borg-drinking

Yang, A. (2022, October 26). Judge dismisses suit alleging TikTok 'blackout challenge' caused girl's death. *NBC News*. Retrieved from https://www.nbcnews.com/news/judge-dismisses-suit-alleging-tiktok-blackout-challenge-caused-girls-d-rcna54208

Chapter 6

Prevention and Intervention Strategies

LEARNING OBJECTIVES

Upon completion of this chapter, you will be able to:

1. Discuss the importance of open communication between parents and children in preventing and addressing cyberbullying.
2. Analyze the role of schools and communities in creating safe and supportive online environments.
3. Identify effective digital hygiene practices to mitigate the risks of cyberbullying and online harassment.
4. Evaluate the impact of empathy training and bystander intervention programs on reducing cyberbullying incidents.

In this chapter, we explore cyberbullying intervention and prevention strategies. Drawing from empirical literature, we emphasize the importance of open communication for parents, which fosters a supportive environment for children to share their online experiences. We also highlight the significance of promoting digital well-being and cultivating positive online spaces, which are crucial for mitigating the impacts of cyberbullying. Additionally, we discuss strategies for creating safe online spaces that empower users to engage respectfully. The role of schools and communities is examined, showcasing how collaborative efforts can effectively combat cyberbullying. Lastly, we will discuss the role of empathy training, bystander training, and example cyberbullying curriculum designs.

OPEN COMMUNICATION

Open communication is vital in addressing cyberbullying among adolescents. Research indicates that parental communication styles significantly influence cyberbullying dynamics. A systematic review by Zhu and colleagues (2021), examining studies from 2015 to 2019, provided insights into these dynamics, highlighting both risk and protective factors related to parental roles.

The review found that aggressive communication from parents is linked to severe cases of cyberbullying, whereas open communication acts as a protective measure. Factors such as parental neglect, abuse, inconsistent supervision of adolescents' online activities, and family dysfunction are associated with heightened risks of cyberbullying. Conversely, active parental involvement, a positive parent-child relationship, and effective communication can enhance children's adaptability at school and reduce the likelihood of cyberbullying. Striking a balance in parental monitoring—combining control with openness—emerges as a key protective factor. However, the review also warns that insufficient or overly controlling parental monitoring can itself become a risk factor (Zhu et al., 2021).

Effective parental intervention in cyberbullying involves building better parent-child relationships through open communication, autonomy-supportive parental control strategies, and enhancing parents' knowledge of internet use and technology (Cao, 2023). Another study by Legate et al. (2019) examined the impact of various parenting strategies on adolescents' involvement in cyberbullying. Analyzing data from over 1,000 parent-child pairs, the research found that autonomy-supportive parenting, which includes understanding the child's perspective and providing rationales for rules, significantly reduces cyberbullying behaviors. Conversely, controlling parenting strategies, especially those involving guilt and shame, tend to increase the likelihood of cyberbullying. The findings emphasize the importance of fostering an environment of autonomy support to mitigate online aggression among adolescents (Legate et al., 2019).

Table 6.1 presents the summary of the findings from the above literature review studies with example strategies.

In addition, adolescents involved in cyberbullying, whether as perpetrators or victims, often have less open and more avoidant communication with their parents compared to those not involved in cyberbullying (Ortega Barón et al., 2018). Open and supportive family communication acts as a protective factor, helping adolescents feel secure enough to discuss and seek help for cyberbullying experiences, thereby reducing its incidence and impact.

Studies have also shown the significant impact of teacher personality on cyberbullying among adolescents. Teachers with strong personal competencies, such as empathy, integrity, and effective communication, play a crucial

Table 6.1 Summary of the Selected Literature on Parental Strategies and Cyberbullying Prevention

Key Findings	Description	Example Strategies
Parental Communication	Open and effective communication between parents and adolescents can reduce the likelihood of cyberbullying involvement.	• Regularly scheduled family meetings to discuss online experiences and address concerns. • Encouraging adolescents to share their feelings and experiences about cyberbullying. • Using role-playing scenarios to help them understand the emotional impact of cyberbullying. • Providing a non-judgmental space for them to talk about their online interactions and seek advice.
Parental Mediation	Autonomy-supportive parenting, involving open discussions and joint rule-setting about internet use, is more effective in preventing cyberbullying than restrictive mediation.	• Implement supervision strategies that respect adolescents' autonomy, such as occasional tracking of online activities without using invasive measures like digital tracking software. • Avoid restrictive mediation focusing solely on limiting access to certain websites or content.
Parental Knowledge	Parents who are well-informed about internet risks and cyberbullying can better guide their children in safe online practices.	• Provide resources and training to parents on digital safety and internet risks to increase their awareness and understanding.

role in mitigating cyberbullying behaviors. The study of Putro and Rachman (2022) reveals a negative correlation between teacher personality competence and the prevalence of cyberbullying, indicating that the higher the teacher's personality competence, the lower the incidence of cyberbullying among students (Putro & Rachman, 2022).

Finally, in their qualitative study, Lynch et al. (2015) explored various actions parents took to support their children through cyberbullying incidents, highlighting a spectrum of responses. Parents often engaged in both direct and indirect actions, such as contacting the bully's parents or the school and even involving the police when necessary. Some parents found success in these confrontations, while others faced resistance, particularly from other parents who refused to acknowledge the severity of the bullying. Additionally, parents monitored their children's online activities, gathering evidence to present to authorities, and sought professional counseling to help their children cope. Despite these efforts, many parents felt frustrated by the lack of decisive action from schools and the emotional toll on their families, emphasizing the need for clearer protocols and supportive measures to effectively address and prevent cyberbullying. These interview findings underscore the critical importance of a unified, collaborative approach involving parents, schools, and law enforcement to protect and support victims of cyberbullying. (Lynch et al., 2015).

DIGITAL HYGIENE

Maintaining good digital hygiene is just as essential as personal hygiene in the physical world. The term "hygiene" originates from Hygieia, the Greek goddess symbolizing health, cleanliness, and sanitation (Rodrigues, 2010). According to Alissa Sklar (2017), digital hygiene involves the safe, healthy, and responsible use of technology in our everyday lives.

Bhandari et al. (2024) conducted a literature review study on digital hygiene and its implications for adolescents, particularly focusing on the risks and preventive measures associated with poor digital practices. The research highlights the critical importance of privacy management, online behavior monitoring, and cybersecurity awareness in maintaining digital hygiene. In addition, the study emphasizes the role of parents and educators in guiding adolescents toward safe online behaviors and underscores the mental health implications of neglecting digital hygiene.

It is important to highlight that neglect of digital hygiene can lead to significant risks such as cyberbullying, online harassment, identity theft, and mental health issues like anxiety and depression (Acheson, 2022). Table 6.2 summarizes strategies identified from the current available empirical literature on strategies for sustaining digital hygiene.

CLASS ACTIVITY: MANAGING DIGITAL FOOTPRINTS

The following activity serves as a sample exercise designed to teach students one of the critical components of digital hygiene: "Managing Digital Footprints." This engaging and interactive activity aims to help students understand the importance of their online presence and the long-term implications of their digital actions. Through a combination of questions, presentations, hands-on demonstrations, and collaborative discussions, students will be able to gain practical skills in assessing and managing their digital footprints.

Table 6.2 A Synthesis of the Key Concepts and Strategies Related to Digital Hygiene

Digital Hygiene Concepts	*Strategies*
Privacy Management	—Use strong, unique passwords for each account.
	—Regularly update privacy settings on social media platforms.
	—Limit sharing of personal information online.
	—Be mindful of location sharing.
	—Log out after use.
	—Regularly review and uninstall apps that you no longer use.
	—Avoid suspicious downloads.
	—Use ad-blockers to reduce exposure to potential dangers.
	—Avoid using public USB charging stations.
Online Behavior Monitoring	—Ensure parental involvement in monitoring and guiding children's digital activities while respecting privacy.
	—Incorporate lessons on digital hygiene into their teaching.
	—Encourage self-monitoring of screen time and setting limits.
	—Promote critical thinking and open communication about online activities.
Mental Health Implications	—Advocate for digital detox and balanced online-offline activities.
	—Engage in outdoor activities to support the benefits of digital detox.
	—Recognize and address digital stress and cyberbullying incidents promptly.
	—Educate about the link between excessive screen time and anxiety/depression.
Cybersecurity Awareness	—Teach how to identify and avoid phishing and online scams.
	—Promote the safe use of cloud services and password managers.
	—Encourage managing digital footprints to prevent oversharing and data breaches.
	—Foster a cybersecurity culture among youth through regular education.
Educational Interventions	—Integrate digital hygiene practices into school curricula and family education programs.
	—Organize workshops and training programs focused on digital literacy.
	—Facilitate collaboration between parents, educators, and tech developers.
	—Develop frameworks for teaching and implementing digital hygiene practices.

(Continued)

Table 6.2 (Continued)

Digital Hygiene Concepts	*Strategies*
Influence of Peers and Social Media	—Address peer pressure and social media influence on digital behavior. —Implement strategies to mitigate negative influences and promote positive interactions online.
Technological Developments	—Stay informed about emerging social media platforms and their impact on youth behavior. —Utilize augmented reality (AR) and VR in digital education. —Apply AI to monitor and enhance digital hygiene.
Cultural and Geographical Variations	—Recognize differences in digital hygiene practices across cultures and regions. —Develop tailored interventions considering cultural contexts.
Digital Literacy and Citizenship	—Teach responsible digital behavior as part of digital citizenship. —Create guidelines and rules with input from children. —Emphasize respectful and civil online interactions. —Address ethical and legal implications of digital activities.
Parental and Family Involvement	—Establish household rules for digital device usage. —Educate children about safe online behavior through active participation. —Develop a family contract for digital citizenship. —Model good digital hygiene practices.
Digital Resilience	—Build resilience to recover from negative online experiences. —Develop comprehensive models including individual, societal, and community interventions. —Ensure access to psychological support and legal frameworks.

Activity Outline

Introduction (5 minutes)

- Have you ever Googled yourself? If so, were you surprised by what you found?
- How much of your personal information is publicly accessible online?
- Do you think your social media profiles reflect the person you are today or the person you want to be in the future?
- What steps can you take to protect your online privacy and reputation?

- Begin with a brief explanation of what a digital footprint is and why it is important.
- Explain the potential long-term consequences of not managing one's digital footprint, including impacts on privacy, reputation, and future opportunities.

Presentation (10 minutes)

- Use a projector to present key points on managing digital footprints:
  - ° Definition of a digital footprint.
  - ° Types of digital footprints (active vs. passive).
  - ° Importance of managing digital footprints.
  - ° Strategies for managing digital footprints.

Interactive Demonstration (10 minutes)

- Demonstrate how to search for one's digital footprint online.
- Show students how to adjust privacy settings on popular social media platforms.
- Provide a checklist of steps for cleaning up their digital footprint, such as deleting old accounts and reviewing past posts.

Group Discussion (5 minutes)

- Divide students into small groups.
- Ask each group to discuss one strategy for managing digital footprints and how they can implement it in their own online activities.
- Have each group share their ideas with the class.

INSTRUCTOR HANDOUT: TIPS FOR MANAGING YOUR DIGITAL FOOTPRINT

Understanding Your Digital Footprint

- **Definition:** Your digital footprint is the trail of data you leave behind when you use the internet.
- **Types:**
  - ° Active: Information you deliberately share (e.g., social media posts).
  - ° Passive: Information collected without your explicit knowledge (e.g., browsing history).

Why It Matters

- **Privacy:** Protects your personal information from misuse.
- **Reputation:** Ensures your online presence reflects positively on you.
- **Opportunities:** Maintains a professional online profile that can benefit future education and career prospects.

Strategies for Managing Your Digital Footprint

1. **Search Yourself Online**
   - Regularly search for your name on search engines to see what information is publicly available.
2. **Privacy Settings**
   - Adjust privacy settings on social media accounts to control who can see your posts and personal information.
3. **Review Past Posts**
   - Go through old social media posts and delete anything that could be seen as inappropriate or unprofessional.
4. **Delete Unused Accounts**
   - Close accounts you no longer use to reduce your online footprint.
5. **Be Mindful of What You Share**
   - Think before you post or share information online. Ask yourself if it's something you'd want future employers or schools to see.
6. **Use Strong Passwords**
   - Protect your accounts with strong, unique passwords to prevent unauthorized access.
7. **Regularly Update Your Privacy Settings**
   - Social media platforms frequently update their privacy settings. Regularly check and update your settings to ensure maximum privacy.

Maintaining a Positive Digital Footprint

- **Professional Profile:** Create and maintain a LinkedIn profile or a personal website that showcases your achievements and skills.
- **Positive Contributions:** Share content that reflects your interests and values positively.
- **Engage Responsibly:** Participate in online discussions and communities respectfully and constructively.

The Role of Schools and Communities

Schools, communities, and support systems are crucial in addressing cyberbullying through prevention, intervention, and mitigation strategies. Addressing cyberbullying requires a collaborative effort that extends beyond the classroom, highlighting the importance of partnership between educational institutions and the broader community. A significant challenge in this effort is the blurred boundaries between home and school, where cyberbullying often spills over, leading to confusion regarding the distinctions between traditional bullying and cyberbullying, as well as a poor understanding of official policies (Su et al., 2021).

The study by Su et al. (2021) explored the experiences of school counselors in collaborating with families to address cyberbullying. Through qualitative interviews with seventeen school counselors, the researchers sought to understand the challenges and strategies involved in these collaborative efforts. Four main themes emerged: the importance of building strong partnerships with parents, the need for digital citizenship education, the challenges of blurred boundaries between home and school, and the necessity for ongoing support and resources. The study highlighted that student deception in hiding online activities was identified as a significant challenge, with students often finding ways to bypass parental controls. For instance, one school counselor noted,

[A student] whose parent did not allow her to have social media, what [did] she do? She signed into her friend's account and used her friend's account all day long. Her mom had no idea, until we talked to mom about it. (Su et al., 2021, p. 5)

Additionally, school counselors stressed the importance of relationship building with parents to ensure a unified approach to combating cyberbullying. Moreover, educating both students and parents about responsible online behavior and internet safety was deemed crucial for prevention.

Similarly, another study conducted by Fu et al. (2021) highlights the importance of collaboration between parents and teachers to effectively address bullying, particularly in under-resourced urban schools. Fu et al. (2021) investigated how children's willingness to share their daily experiences with their parents (child disclosure) and effective communication between parents and teachers (parent-teacher connection) impact bullying behaviors. Child disclosure refers to children voluntarily sharing their daily activities and experiences with their parents. The researchers collected data from 110 fourth and fifth graders and their parents in two urban schools. The findings revealed that child disclosure alone was not sufficient to reduce bullying. However, when there was a strong parent-teacher connection, children who disclosed more information to their parents exhibited less relational and cyberbullying.

The study by Chen et al. (2023) highlighted the significance of building strong, supportive relationships within families and communities to equip adolescents with the social resources needed to respond effectively to cyberbullying. Data were collected from 1207 students in grades seven–nine from boarding schools in rural China using questionnaires. The findings showed that cyberbullying victims communicated less frequently with their parents compared to non-victims. Participants with higher levels of offline social capital, including strong family bonds, peer relationships, and school support, were more likely to defend cyberbullying victims. Conversely, those with more online social capital were more passive in their bystander reactions.

Furthermore, the study by Gámez-Guadix et al. (2015) aimed to understand the dynamics of cyberbullying among adolescents and identify effective prevention strategies. Conducted in Bizkaia, Spain, it involved 969 adolescents aged thirteen to eighteen from twelve randomly selected secondary schools. The study found that comprehensive cyberbullying prevention programs within the school curriculum, clear policies, and community initiatives such as awareness-raising campaigns and workshops significantly contribute to reducing cyberbullying. The researchers emphasized the importance of strong family and community engagement, recommending that schools adopt whole-school anti-cyberbullying policies involving students, parents, and community members.

In addressing cyberbullying, school personnel should take a proactive approach as suggested by Mason (2008). This involves understanding the dynamics of cyberbullying, holding perpetrators accountable, empowering bystanders to intervene, educating students on the impact of cyberbullying, and enforcing clear anti-cyberbullying policies. Based on these recommendations, I have developed a sample anti-bullying policy statement for schools to adopt and implement. The definitions provided in the policy were compiled from the work of Azumah et al. (2023).

EXAMPLE ANTI-CYBERBULLYING POLICY AND ACTION STATEMENT

Mission

Our school is committed to providing a safe and inclusive environment for all students. We believe that every student has the right to feel safe and respected, both offline and online. We are dedicated to preventing and responding to all forms of bullying, including cyberbullying, and fostering a culture of respect and inclusion.

Definitions

Cyberbullying: Cyberbullying is the use of electronic communication to bully a person, typically by sending messages of an intimidating or threatening nature. Some significant forms of cyberbullying include:

- ✓ **Harassment:** Repeatedly sending offensive, insulting, and hurtful messages over the internet.
- ✓ **Flaming:** Engaging in heated online exchanges where participants use rude, offensive, and threatening language via emails, instant messaging, and social media.
- ✓ **Stalking:** Consistently using the internet or social media to pursue, threaten, or physically harm individuals, causing them to feel unsafe.
- ✓ **Denigration:** Spreading defamatory information about a person online to humiliate or damage their reputation.
- ✓ **Impersonation:** Pretending to be someone else online to damage their reputation or deceive others into disliking them.
- ✓ **Outing:** Publicly sharing someone's private information or secrets online without their consent.
- ✓ **Trickery:** Deceiving someone into revealing personal information, which is then shared without their approval.
- ✓ **Trolling:** Engaging in disruptive online behavior aimed at upsetting or harming others, though definitions may vary.
- ✓ **Exclusion:** Deliberately excluding someone from an online group or community.
- ✓ **Doxing:** Releasing someone's confidential or sensitive information online without their consent, potentially leading to harm.
- ✓ **Masquerading:** Using a fake identity online to harass or harm others without revealing one's true identity.
- ✓ **Hate Crime:** Bullying motivated by prejudice against someone's race, religion, sexual orientation, gender, disability, or ethnicity.

Roles and Responsibilities

- **Students:** Expected to uphold school values, report bullying, and refrain from participating in any form of bullying.
- **Staff:** Act as role models, take all accusations seriously, enforce policies, and participate in training on bullying prevention.
- **Parents:** Respect school rules, support staff, communicate regularly, and encourage their children to speak up about bullying.

- **Bystanders:** Responsible for intervening and reporting bullying incidents.
- **Leadership:** Form a bullying committee to keep the policy updated and handle escalated incidents.

Procedures

Reporting and Response:

✓ All incidents of bullying should be reported immediately to the principal or designated staff member.
✓ Each report will be promptly investigated, and appropriate actions will be taken based on the findings.
✓ Consequences for bullying may include counseling, detention, suspension, or other disciplinary actions.

Prevention Strategies:
Our school will:

✓ **Conduct** regular training sessions for staff and students to help them recognize and prevent bullying in the form of annual workshops and refresher courses on the latest bullying prevention techniques.
✓ **Integrate** digital citizenship and empathy lessons into the curriculum to promote respectful and responsible online behavior. This will include adding specific modules on digital etiquette and the impacts of cyberbullying to existing subjects.

Support Systems:
Our school will:

✓ **Offer** counseling and support resources for students who have been victims of bullying.
✓ **Implement** restorative practices to address the harm caused by bullying. Facilitating meetings between victims and perpetrators to promote understanding and healing and using conflict resolution techniques to rebuild trust.
✓ **Create** a safe reporting environment for students to feel comfortable reporting bullying incidents. This can involve setting up anonymous reporting systems and regular check-ins with students.

Teachers should discuss this policy with their students in age-appropriate ways and assure them that they need not endure any form of bullying. Students who bully are in violation of the school's anti-bullying policy and will be subject to disciplinary action.

HASHTAGS FOR DIGITAL COMMUNITY SUPPORT

Social media can be a powerful platform for raising awareness, educating, and promoting action against cyberbullying through the use of targeted hashtags. I have compiled some of the popular ones here:

- #DigitalCitizenship: Promotes responsible and ethical behavior online, guiding individuals to navigate the digital world safely.
- #EndTheHate: Aims to eliminate hate speech and foster a more inclusive digital space.
- #SupportNotSilence: Encourages support for victims of cyberbullying, promoting empathy and action.
- #ThinkBeforeYouPost: Reminds users to consider the impact of their words before posting.
- #BeKindOnline: Promotes kindness and respect in online interactions.
- #KindnessIsCool: Highlights that being kind online is both important and "cool."
- #BeAnAlly: Urges individuals to stand up for those being bullied and offer support.
- #RaiseYourVoice: Encourages speaking out against cyberbullying and advocating for change.
- #BeTheChange: Promotes personal responsibility and positive online interactions.
- #SpeakUp: Supports those affected by cyberbullying and fosters a community of support.
- #CompassionOverCruelty: Advocates for compassion and kindness in online interactions.
- #StopTheStigma: Aims to reduce the stigma surrounding mental health issues related to bullying.
- #StopTheCycle: Calls to break the cycle of bullying behavior, promoting healing and understanding.
- #YouAreNotAlone: Offers support to those experiencing cyberbullying, reminding them they are not alone.

If you are reading this section, can you join the movement and post something using the hashtag #SupportNotSilence?

EMPATHY TRAINING

The term "empathy" is generally understood as a multidimensional concept. It can be categorized into two main types: affective empathy and cognitive empathy. Affective empathy refers to the capacity to share and experience the emotions of others, meaning one feels what another person feels emotionally (Decety, 2010). Cognitive empathy, on the other hand, refers to understanding another's perspective without necessarily sharing their emotions (Decety & Cowell, 2015).

Empathy training is a crucial component in addressing cyberbullying among adolescents. High levels of empathy have been associated with lower levels of cyberbullying perpetration (Yang et al., 2020). High levels of empathy have been associated with lower levels of cyberbullying perpetration (Yang et al., 2020). Furthermore, emotion regulation, which is intrinsically connected to empathy, plays a crucial role in disrupting the cycle of cyberbullying (Mujidin et al., 2023).

In their study on cyberbullying, Ang and Goh (2010) examine the roles of both affective and cognitive empathy among adolescents. They found that both types of empathy are important in understanding and addressing cyberbullying behaviors, with affective empathy being particularly significant in reducing such behaviors among boys, while for girls, high levels of affective empathy seem to buffer the effects of low cognitive empathy (Ang & Goh, 2010).

Empirical literature emphasizes the role of virtual reality (VR) in empathy training by creating immersive environments that facilitate perspective-taking through body ownership illusions (Trivedi-Bateman & Crook, 2021). For example, the study of Peck and colleagues (2013) aimed to investigate whether embodying light-skinned participants in a dark-skinned virtual body could reduce implicit racial bias. Participants, university students, were divided into groups with different virtual bodies: light-skinned, dark-skinned, non-embodied dark-skinned, and purple-skinned. Using the Implicit Association Test (IAT) to measure racial bias before and after the VR experience, the findings revealed that those embodied in dark-skinned avatars showed a significant reduction in implicit racial bias compared to other groups (Peck et al., 2013).

Similarly, the study by Bertrand et al. (2018) utilized VR to create body ownership illusions, allowing participants to experience scenarios from another person's perspective. Participants underwent several VR sessions designed to evoke empathic responses by placing them in different social situations. They measured empathy through pre- and post-test assessments using validated empathy scales, questionnaires, and behavioral observations. This approach enabled the researchers to assess changes in empathy-related abilities, including perspective-taking, compassion, and affective empathy.

Teachers and school counselors are encouraged to incorporate empathy training into their cyberbullying prevention strategies to create a more empathetic school environment and reduce instances of cyberbullying (Salem et al., 2023). In a study by Salem et al. (2023), 217 middle school students in Egypt, were divided into experimental and control groups. The experimental group received cognitive-behavioral therapy focused on enhancing empathy. The training consisted of twenty sessions, utilizing various counseling methods such as discussion and dialogue, feedback, storytelling, role-playing, exercises, fun and humor, imaginary modeling, live modeling, positive reinforcement, brainstorming, and homework. Post-intervention assessments showed significant improvements in empathy and reductions in cyberbullying behaviors among the experimental group, with positive effects maintained at a two-month follow-up (Salem et al., 2023).

Empathy training examples range from experiential methods to cognitive and behavioral approaches, with applications in various fields such as medical education and healthcare. Below, three examples empathy training activities have been presented.

ACTIVITY 1: INTRODUCTION TO EMPATHY

Learning Objectives

Upon completion of this activity, you will be able to:

- Define empathy and its types.
- Discuss the role of empathy in social interactions.
- Reflect on personal experiences of empathy in an online journal.

To-Do List:
Watch: "What is Empathy?" Video [Link to a YouTube video]
Discuss the following questions:

- What does empathy mean to you?
- Can you recall a time when you felt someone was empathetic toward you?
- Why do you think empathy is important in our daily lives and interactions with others?
- What are some ways we can show empathy to others, especially in online interactions?
- How can we improve our ability to empathize with others?

ACTIVITY 2: UNDERSTANDING CYBERBULLYING

Learning Objectives

Upon completion of this activity, you will be able to:

- Identify different forms of cyberbullying.
- Understand the emotional impact of cyberbullying on victims.
- Develop strategies to prevent and respond to cyberbullying.

To-Do List:
Watch: "Understanding Cyberbullying." [Link to a YouTube video]
Discuss the following questions:

- What emotions do victims of cyberbullying experience?
- Why is it important to address cyberbullying?
- What strategies can we use to prevent and respond to cyberbullying?
- How can empathy play a role in combating cyberbullying?

Role-Playing Activity:

- Participate in role-playing scenarios that depict different forms of cyberbullying.
- Reflect on the emotions and perspectives of both the victim and the perpetrator.

Scenario 1: Social Media Harassment
Description: Alex posts a photo on social media. Jamie, who feels jealous of Alex's popularity, starts posting hurtful comments under the photo and encourages others to do the same.
Roles:
- **Alex:** Expresses feelings of hurt, confusion, and isolation.
- **Jamie:** Acts out jealousy and desire to bring Alex down.
- **Bystanders:** Respond in different ways, either joining in, defending Alex, or staying silent.
Reflection Questions:
- How did Alex feel when reading the comments?
- What motivated Jamie to post the hurtful comments?
- How did the actions of the bystanders affect the situation?
- What could Jamie and the bystanders have done differently?

Scenario 2: Anonymous Threats
Description: Sam receives anonymous threatening messages through a messaging app, telling them to stop participating in an online forum. Sam is scared and doesn't know who is behind the threats.
Roles:
- **Sam:** Shows fear, anxiety, and reluctance to go online.
- **Anonymous Bully:** Sends threatening messages with the intent to intimidate.
- **Friend:** Sam confides in a friend who reacts in various supportive or unsupportive ways.
Reflection Questions:
- What impact did the threats have on Sam's emotional state?
- Why might someone choose to send anonymous threats?
- How can Sam's friend best support them in this situation?
- What steps can Sam take to address cyberbullying?

Scenario 3: Exclusion from Online Group

Description: Taylor is part of an online gaming group. After a disagreement, several group members decide to exclude Taylor from the group's activities and chats, spreading rumors about Taylor in the process.

Roles:

- **Taylor (Victim):** Experiences feelings of exclusion, loneliness, and betrayal.
- **Group Members (Perpetrators):** Justify their actions and spread rumors.
- **Moderator:** Tries to mediate the situation and decide on appropriate actions.

Reflection Questions:

- How did the exclusion affect Taylor's sense of belonging and self-esteem?
- What reasons did the group members have for excluding Taylor?
- How effective was the moderator's intervention?
- What could have been done to prevent the situation from escalating?

Scenario 4: Forwarding Embarrassing Photos

Description: Jordan shares a funny but embarrassing photo of themselves with a close friend, Casey. Casey forwards the photo to others without Jordan's permission, leading to widespread ridicule.

Roles:

- **Jordan (Victim):** Feels embarrassed, betrayed, and humiliated.
- **Casey (Perpetrator):** Acts out of thoughtlessness or seeking approval from others.
- **Receivers:** React to the photo in various ways, either laughing, expressing concern, or ignoring it.

Reflection Questions:

- How did Jordan feel when they found out the photo was shared?
- What motivated Casey to forward the photo?
- How did the receivers' reactions impact Jordan?
- What responsibilities do friends have when sharing personal content?

ACTIVITY 3: ENHANCING AFFECTIVE EMPATHY

Learning Objectives

Upon completion of this activity, you will be able to:

- Recognize and articulate personal and others' emotions.
- Develop and practice compassion toward others.
- Reflect on the impact of affective empathy in daily interactions.

Discussion Questions:

HOW DO YOU FEEL IN DIFFERENT SITUATIONS?

- Example: Describe a time when you felt nervous before a big exam. What were the physical and emotional signs of your nervousness?

WHY IS IT IMPORTANT TO RECOGNIZE OTHERS' EMOTIONS?

• Example: Recall an instance where you noticed a friend was upset even though they didn't say anything. How did recognizing their emotions help you support them?

CREATING EMPATHY MAP

Empathy maps help in understanding others' emotions and perspectives. A typical empathy map includes sections for "Says," "Thinks," "Does," and "Feels."

Read the following scenario: "*Ayse shared a funny photo in disappearing mode with her close friend group. One of her friends took a screenshot and shared it in a large WhatsApp class group without her permission. Ayse is now facing a mix of emotions.*"

Fill out the empathy map for Ayse, discussing and writing down what Ayse might be: (see figure 6.1)

- **Says:** "I feel so alone here."
- **Thinks:** "Will I ever make friends?"
- **Does:** "Avoiding using WhatsApp."
- **Feels:** "Lonely, anxious, overwhelmed."

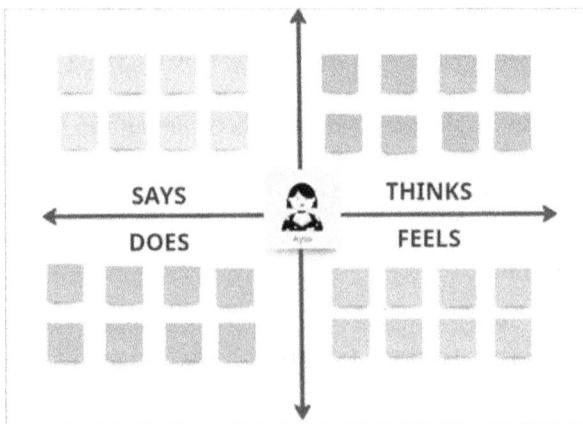

Figure 6.1 An Empathy Training Mind Map. *Source*: Author generated using Canva.com.

BYSTANDER TRAINING

The bystander effect is a social psychological phenomenon where the presence of others reduces an individual's likelihood to help in emergencies. Individuals are less likely to offer help to a victim when other people are present, and the probability of intervention decreases as the number of bystanders increases (Fischer et al., 2011). This effect is often attributed to diffusion of responsibility, where each bystander assumes someone else will take action, and social influence, where people look to others for cues on how to behave.

Previous literature indicated that many cyberbullying intervention programs and research focus on education, coping skills, communication, bystander, and digital citizenship. However, there is a growing recognition of the importance of including "bystander training" in these initiatives (Doumas & Midgett, 2022).

The Bystander Intervention Model (BIM), proposed by Latané and Darley in 1970, was developed to analyze bystander behavior in emergency situations. It outlines five sequential phases that an individual must go through to intervene, as described in figure 6.2.

The first phase, *Noticing the Event*, involves becoming aware that something significant is happening. It is the initial step where a bystander detects an unusual or troubling event. The second phase, *Interpreting the Event*, requires the bystander to recognize the situation as an emergency or one that requires intervention. This involves assessing the seriousness and urgency of the event. In the third phase, *Assuming Responsibility*, the bystander decides that they have a personal responsibility to act, overcoming the diffusion of responsibility that often occurs in group settings. The fourth phase, *Deciding How to Intervene*, involves understanding what actions are necessary and how to help effectively. This requires the bystander to have or seek out the knowledge and skills needed to provide assistance. The final phase, *Implementing Intervention Decisions*, involves taking action to intervene, whether it is directly intervening or seeking help from others.

The study of Ferreira et al. (2019) investigates the relationship between the phases of the BIM and the role of self-efficacy beliefs in influencing bystander behaviors in cyberbullying situations. The study involved 676 students from fifth to twelfth grade, who responded to questionnaires assessing various aspects of bystander behavior and self-efficacy in the context of cyberbullying. The findings showed that self-efficacy significantly influences bystander behavior, with higher self-efficacy linked to more proactive and positive interventions (Ferreira et al., 2019).

Now, the question arises: what are the strategies to intervene in cyberbullying? Midgett et al. (2015) introduced the STAC program, which stands

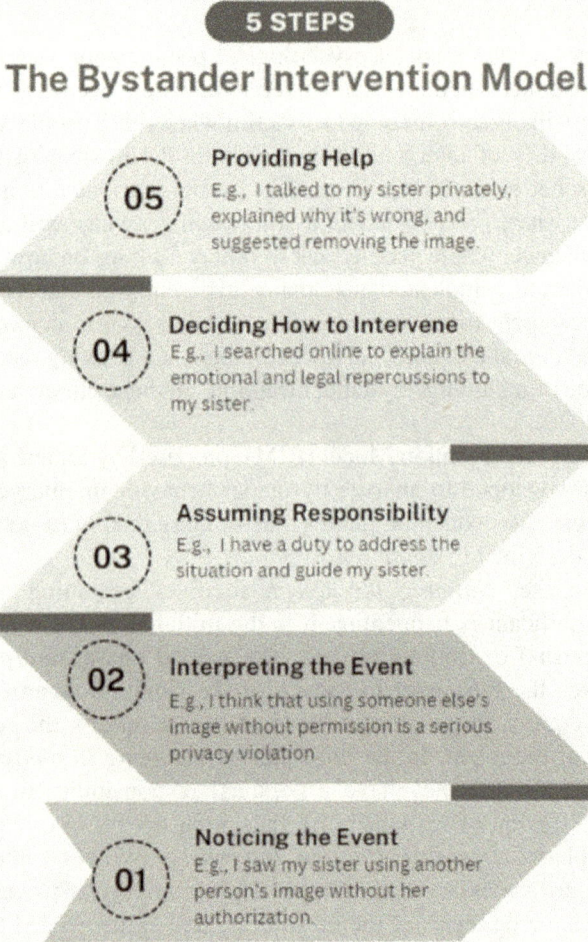

Figure 6.2 The Steps of the Bystander Intervention Model (BIM). *Source*: Author generated using Canva.com.

for "Stealing the Show," "Turning it Over," "Accompanying Others," and "Coaching Compassion." This brief bystander intervention aims to empower individuals to effectively address and mitigate bullying behaviors. The table below provides definitions and examples of each strategy. (See table 6.3)

Using the STAC program, Doumas, Midgett, and Watts (2019) worked with sixty-five high school students to evaluate the validity of the STAC

Table 6.3 Bystander Intervention Strategies (Midgett et al., 2015)

Strategy	Description	Example
Stealing the Show	Divert attention away from the bullying situation to de-escalate it.	When you see someone being bullied in the hallway, start a conversation with the bully about an unrelated topic to distract them.
Turning it Over	Report the bullying incident to a trusted adult or authority figure.	After witnessing bullying in the cafeteria, go to a teacher or school counselor to report the incident.
Accompanying Others	Support the victim by staying with them and offering comfort.	Sit with the victim during lunch and offer your company, letting them know they are not alone.
Coaching Compassion	Encourage empathy and understanding among peers to reduce bullying.	Talk to your friends about how the victim might feel and suggest ways they can be more supportive and inclusive.

training. Results showed that the majority of students found the program acceptable and relevant. Participants in the intervention group reported significant increases in their knowledge and confidence to intervene in bullying situations. However, despite being trained in all four intervention strategies, students used "Accompanying Others" and "Coaching Compassion" most frequently, while "Stealing the Show" and "Turning it Over" were used less often.

ROLE-PLAYING ACTIVITY: "WHICH STRATEGY WOULD YOU USE TO PREVENT?"

Scenario: You and your friends are relaxing at your place after school, scrolling through Instagram. One of your friends stumbles upon a classmate's recent story where they proudly share their new hobby, painting. Your friend starts laughing and saves the story. Without hesitation, they screenshot it, add a mocking caption ("Look at this wannabe Picasso, LOL!"), and share it in your group chat, encouraging everyone to comment with derogatory remarks (see figure 6.3). This friend has a history of belittling others' interests and activities on social media.

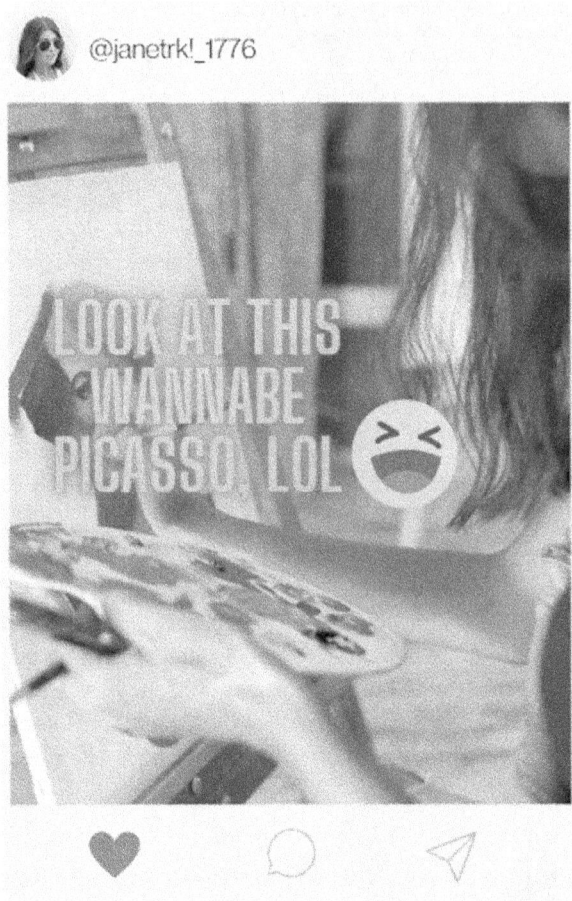

Figure 6.3 Example of Cyberbullying Activity. *Source*: Author generated using Canva.com.

Instructions:

1. Divide into Groups:
   - Split the class into small groups of four to five students.
   - Assign roles within each group: the friend who mocks, the victim (classmate who shared the painting), bystanders (other friends in the group chat), and an observer.
2. Role-Play:
   - Act out the scenario with each student playing their assigned role.
   - Focus on how each character might feel and react in this situation.

- ◦ Pay attention to the emotions and dynamics at play.
3. Discussion:
    - ◦ After the role-play, discuss the following questions as a group:
        - ▪ How did the victim feel when their painting was mocked and shared without permission?
        - ▪ What might have motivated the friend to mock the painting and encourage derogatory remarks?
        - ▪ How did the bystanders feel, and what were their possible reactions?
        - ▪ What could each person in the scenario have done differently to prevent or stop the cyberbullying?
        - ▪ **Which STAC strategy would you use to intervene?** (Stealing the Show, Turning it Over, Accompanying Others, Coaching Compassion)

Finally, a 2015 study by Patterson et al. (2015) investigated adolescent perceptions of bystanders' responses to cyberbullying. Using vignette-guided interviews with twenty-four students aged thirteen to sixteen from Australia, the study sought to understand the factors influencing bystander behavior in online bullying scenarios (Patterson et al., 2015). The vignette-guided method includes presenting participants with short, descriptive stories of cyberbullying incidents to elicit their opinions, attitudes, and beliefs about the content.

The findings highlighted that the likelihood of bystander intervention is heavily influenced by the relationships between the bystander and the victim or perpetrator, the severity of the incident, and the presence of other bystanders. Additionally, the study revealed a reluctance among adolescents to involve adults, preferring instead to seek advice from peers (Patterson et al., 2015). The research concluded that empowering bystanders through targeted interventions could significantly reduce cyberbullying.

In conclusion, the breadth of current research on "bystander training" highlights a pivotal strategy in combating cyberbullying: empowering bystanders through well-designed intervention programs. Empowered with higher self-efficacy and practical strategies, individuals can transform from passive observers into proactive defenders. As informed by the empirical studies, this transformation not only mitigates bullying behaviors but also fosters a culture of empathy and support, creating safer and more inclusive online environments.

ANTI-CYBERBULLYING CURRICULUM DESIGN EXAMPLES

In this section, I will examine several anti-bullying resources to analyze their curriculum designs, teaching activities, and learning materials. My purpose is to synthesize their instructional approaches, highlighting best practices and strategies in anti-cyberbullying education.

BULLIESOUT

One notable example is BulliesOut (https://bulliesout.com/about-bulliesout/), a UK-based anti-bullying charity, which offers resources including workshops, e-mentoring, blog articles, and courses. Their interactive workshops cover essential topics such as changing attitudes, challenging stereotypes, online bullying, sexting, online safety, digital footprint, respectful relationships, positive friendships, and kindness.

Additionally, BulliesOut offers e-mentoring programs with paid courses on "Positive Behavior in the Workplace," "Dealing Effectively with Bullying and Harassment," "Understanding and Exploring Bullying for Professionals," and "Online Safety for Parents and Educators."

The site also offers a wide range of blog articles under their "Help & Information" section, which includes topics for young people, parents, workplaces, and school staff to provide information about various current terminologies such as gaslighting, catfishing, ghosting, doxing, screen time addiction, password protection, and so on.

The best feature of this site is its language. It explains content for different audiences and age groups effectively by including supplemental free animated instructional videos that can be integrated into courses to enhance understanding and engagement. These videos cover topics such as "Am I Being Bullied?" "Be Mindful of Your Online Behavior," "Be Kind Online," "No Matter How, No Matter Where, Bullying is not okay!" These videos provide visual and practical examples of the concepts taught, making the learning experience more interactive and impactful.

CYBERBULLYING RESEARCH CENTER

The Cyberbullying Research Center (https://cyberbullying.org/) offers an extensive range of resources aimed at identifying, preventing, and responding to cyberbullying. Their site provides free scripts for parents and teachers to encourage open communication, which is a standout feature. These scripts can be very helpful in initiating conversations about cyberbullying and digital safety.

The site includes sections on:

- **Research:** Empirical studies and statistics on cyberbullying, including reports on trends among different age groups and demographics.
- **Resources:** Guides and toolkits for parents, educators, and students, including strategies to combat cyberbullying and enhance digital safety.

- **Laws and Policies:** Detailed information about bullying and cyberbullying laws across the United States, helping users understand the legal framework and protections available.
- **Presentations:** Tailored presentations for various audiences such as K–12 students, educators, law enforcement, and parents, aiming to raise awareness and provide actionable strategies.
- **Stories:** Personal stories from individuals affected by cyberbullying, offering real-life insights and perspectives.
- **Help and Reporting:** Step-by-step guidance on how to report cyberbullying incidents and seek help, including contact information for various platforms and services.

The Cyberbullying Research Center's comprehensive approach and rich array of resources make it an invaluable tool for those seeking to understand and combat cyberbullying effectively.

Another notable feature is their collaboration with corporations, government agencies, social media platforms, entertainment entities, and non-profits. Partners include Google, X, TikTok, Snapchat, Meta, Instagram, The White House, the FBI, the National PTA, the National Crime Prevention Council, the National Association for Independent Schools, the National District Attorneys Association, TEDx, Scholastic, Fulbright, and the Boys & Girls Clubs of America, among others.

COMMON SENSE EDUCATION

Next, the "Teacher's Essential Guide to Cyberbullying Prevention" by Common Sense Education provides a framework to help educators understand, identify, and combat cyberbullying in schools. This guide addresses several critical areas:

- What is Cyberbullying?: Defines cyberbullying and explains its various forms, including catfishing, cyberflashing, ghosting, griefing, hate pages, and outing.
- Prevalence of Cyberbullying: Provides data and statistics on how common cyberbullying is among teens, highlighting the different impacts on various demographic groups.
- Identifying Cyberbullying: Offers guidance on recognizing signs that a student might be experiencing or engaging in cyberbullying.

- Intervention Strategies: Outlines when and how teachers should intervene in cyberbullying situations, emphasizing the importance of involving families and adhering to school policies.
- Teacher Responsibilities: Explains the role of teachers in preventing cyberbullying, including promoting a positive classroom culture, embracing teachable moments, and incorporating cyberbullying lessons into existing curricula.
- Lesson Plans and Resources: Provides specific lesson plans and classroom activities for different grade levels, from K–12, to teach students about cyberbullying and encourage them to be upstanders.
- Working with Families: Offers strategies for engaging with parents and caregivers to prevent and address cyberbullying, including sharing resources and initiating open communication.

Common Sense Education's training strategy focuses on making sure stakeholders fully understand what cyberbullying is, including its different forms and how common it is among students. The curriculum promotes empathy and positive online behavior, encouraging students to support victims and stand up to bullies. Practical tips are provided for teachers on how to intervene in cyberbullying situations and involve parents effectively. The lesson plans are designed to fit easily into subjects like social studies and digital citizenship, making it simple for teachers to incorporate these important lessons into their everyday teaching. Additionally, Common Sense Education emphasizes the importance of using teachable moments to address issues as they arise, ensuring that discussions about cyberbullying are relevant and timely.

The analysis of existing successful implementations suggests that developing a training or online course for K–12 students on cyberbullying would be highly beneficial. Such a course should begin with a clear definition of cyberbullying, ensuring students understand what constitutes online bullying. It is crucial to highlight the unique characteristics of online bullying, emphasizing how it differs from traditional face-to-face bullying and why it can be more pervasive and harder to escape.

Special attention should be given to how online bullying affects disabled young people and those with special educational needs (SEN), ensuring inclusivity and awareness of the additional challenges these groups may face. The course should also cover the legal aspects of online bullying, helping students understand the potential consequences and protections under the law.

Finally, providing strategies for preventing and responding to cyberbullying will empower students to create a safer online environment and effectively support peers who may be targeted.

"REFLECT AND REFRAME" FOR ADULTS

1. What do you understand when you hear "open communication?" Think of an example from your own experience and discuss how it might influence a child's ability to cope with cyberbullying.
2. How can schools and communities effectively collaborate to create safer online spaces for students?
3. Reflect on your own digital hygiene practices. Provide examples of changes you might implement.
4. Have you ever witnessed or intervened in a cyberbullying incident? Describe the situation and the strategies you used. How effective were they, and what could have been done differently?
5. How can empathy training programs change the behavior of potential cyberbullies and bystanders? Share an example of how empathy training has impacted you or someone you know.

"REFLECT AND REFRAME" FOR KIDS

1. What does "talking openly" mean? For example, telling a teacher if someone is being mean online. How can this help stop bullying?
2. How can schools and families help make the internet safer for kids?
3. How do you keep yourself safe online? For example, not sharing your password. What else can you do to be safer?
4. Have you ever seen someone being bullied online and tried to help? What did you do, like tell a grown-up, and did it help?
5. How can learning to be kind help stop bullies? For example, saying nice things to others. Can you think of a time when being kind helped you or a friend?

REFERENCES

Acheson, R. (2022). Research digest: Digital technology and its impact on child mental health. *Journal of Child Psychotherapy*, *48*(3), 422–435.

Ang, R. P., & Goh, D. H. (2010). Cyberbullying among adolescents: The role of affective and cognitive empathy, and gender. *Child Psychiatry and Human Development*, *41*(4), 387–397. https://doi.org/10.1007/s10578-010-0176-3

Azumah, S. W., Elsayed, N., ElSayed, Z., & Ozer, M. (2023). Cyberbullying in text content detection: An analytical review. *International Journal of Computers and Applications*, *45*(9), 579–586.

Bertrand, P., Guegan, J., Robieux, L., McCall, C. A., & Zenasni, F. (2018). Learning empathy through virtual reality: Multiple strategies for training empathy-related abilities using body ownership illusions in embodied virtual reality. *Frontiers in Robotics and AI*, *5*, 26. https://doi.org/10.3389/frobt.2018.00026

Bhandari, Y., Sree, S. N., Kakar, H., & Malhotra, A. (2024). Literature survey on neglecting digital hygiene: Understanding youth behaviour and its impact. *Annual Research Journal of SCMS, Pune, 12*, 47–67.

Cao, L. (2023). What can parents do with cyberbullying among adolescents? *International Journal of Social Science and Humanity*, *13*(4), 230–236. https://doi.org/10.18178/ijssh.2023.v13.1150

Chen, Q., Xiao, Q., Liu, B., & Lu, Z. (2024). Bystander reaction differences between cyberbullying victims and non-victims among Chinese adolescents: The roles of online and offline social capitals. *Child & Family Social Work*, *29*(2), 354–362.

Decety, J. (2010). The neurodevelopment of empathy in humans. *Developmental Neuroscience*, *32*(4), 257–267. https:doi.org/10.1159/000317771

Decety, J., & Cowell, J. M. (2015). Empathy, justice, and moral behavior. *AJOB Neuroscience*, *6*(3), 3–14. https://doi.org/10.1080/21507740.2015.1047055

Doumas, D. M., Midgett, A., & Watts, A. D. (2019). A pilot evaluation of the social validity of a bullying bystander program adapted for high school students. *Psychology in the Schools*, *56*(7), 1101–1116. https://doi.org/10.1002/pits.22249

Ferreira, P. C., Simão, A. V., Paiva, A., & Ferreira, A. (2020). Responsive bystander behaviour in cyberbullying: A path through self-efficacy. *Behaviour & Information Technology*, *39*(5), 511–524.

Fischer, P., Krueger, J. I., Greitemeyer, T., Vogrincic, C., Kastenmüller, A., Frey, D., & Kainbacher, M. (2011). The bystander-effect: A meta-analytic review on bystander intervention in dangerous and non-dangerous emergencies. *Psychological Bulletin*, *137*(4), 517.

Fu, R., Waasdorp, T. E., Paskewich, B., & Leff, S. S. (2021). Bullying perpetration among youth: The contributions of child disclosure and parent–teacher connection. *Journal of Family Psychology*, *35*(3), 410.

Gámez-Guadix, M., Gini, G., & Calvete, E. (2015). Stability of cyberbullying victimization among adolescents: Prevalence and association with bully–victim status and psychosocial adjustment. *Computers in Human Behavior*, *53*, 140–148.

Latané, B., & Darley, J. M. (1970). *The unresponsive bystander: Why doesn't he help?* New York: Appleton-Century-Crofts.

Legate, N., Weinstein, N., & Przybylski, A. K. (2019). Parenting strategies and adolescents' cyberbullying behaviors: Evidence from a preregistered study of parent–child dyads. *Journal of Youth and Adolescence*, *48*, 399–409.

Lynch, T. E., Green, V. A., Bowden, C., & Harcourt, S. (2015). Why our family? Parental responses to cyberbullying. *Kairaranga*, *16*(1), 7–19.

Midgett, A., Doumas, D. M., Sears, D., Lunquist, A., & Hausheer, R. (2015). A bystander bullying psychoeducation program with middle school students: A preliminary report. *The Professional Counselor*, *5*, 486–500. https://doi.org/10 .15241/am.5.4.486

Mujidin, M., Nuryoto, S., Rustam, H. K., Hildaratri, A., & Echoh, D. U. (2023). The role of emotion regulation and empathy in students displaying cyberbullying. *Humanitas: Indonesian Psychological Journal*, *20*(1), 21–28. https://doi.org/10 .26555/humanitas.v20i1.72

Ortega Barón, J., Postigo, J., Iranzo, B., Buelga, S., & Carrascosa, L. (2018). Parental communication and feelings of affiliation in adolescent aggressors and victims of cyberbullying. *Social Sciences*, *8*(1), 3.

Patterson, L. J., Allan, A., & Cross, D. (2017). Adolescent perceptions of bystanders' responses to cyberbullying. *New Media & Society*, *19*(3), 366–383.

Peck, T. C., Seinfeld, S., Aglioti, S. M., & Slater, M. (2013). Putting yourself in the skin of a black avatar reduces implicit racial bias. *Consciousness and Cognition*, *22*(3), 779–787. https://doi.org/10.1016/j.concog.2013.04.016

Putro, H. Y. S., & Rachman, A. (2022). The relationship of teachers' personal competencies and parents' permissive patterns with adolescent cyberbullying behavior. *Bisma The Journal of Counseling*, *6*(1), 8–15. Retrieved from http://digitalhygiene .com/2010/11/04/what-is-digital-hygiene/

Rodrigues, R. (2010, November 4). What is digital hygiene? *DigitalHygiene.com.*

Sklar, A. (2017). Sound, smart, and safe: A plea for teaching good digital hygiene. *Learning Landscapes*, *10*(2), 39–43.

Su, Y. W., Doty, J., Polley, B. R., Cakmakci, H., Swank, J., & Sickels, A. (2021). Collaborating with families to address cyberbullying: Exploring school counselors' lived experiences. *Professional School Counseling*, *25*(1), 2156759X211053825

Trivedi-Bateman, N., & Crook, E. L. (2022). The optimal application of empathy interventions to reduce antisocial behaviour and crime: A review of the literature. *Psychology, Crime & Law*, *28*(8), 796–819.

Yang, J., Li, W., Ling, G., & Wang, X. (2020). How is trait anger related to adolescents' cyberbullying perpetration? A moderated mediation analysis. *Journal of Interpersonal Violence*, *37*(9–10), NP6633–NP6654. https://doi.org/10.1177 /0886260520967129

Zhu, C., Huang, S., Evans, R., & Zhang, W. (2021). Cyberbullying among adolescents and children: A comprehensive review of the global situation, risk factors, and preventive measures. *Frontiers in Public Health*, *9*, 1–12. https://doi.org/10 .3389/fpubh.2021.634909

About the Author

Merve Basdogan serves as an assistant professor of Instructional Technology within the Department of Curriculum and Instruction at the College of Education, Texas Tech University. She obtained her PhD in Instructional Systems Technology, with a minor in Educational Psychology, from Indiana University (IU) in 2021. Her doctoral research took a critical post-phenomenological approach to examining open and distance education concepts, with the primary aim of advocating for sustainable terminology usage in the educational technology sphere.

In her postdoctoral role with the Learning Spaces and Mosaic Initiative at the University Information Technology Service (UITS) unit of IU, Dr. Basdogan explored innovative, technology-enhanced learning environments. These environments were designed to facilitate active, interactive, flexible, collaborative, and personalized learning experiences, both in formal and informal educational settings.

Prior to joining the faculty at TTU C&I, Merve contributed her expertise as the principal instructional designer and multimedia production specialist at the IU School of Public Health, Office of Online Education. In this role, she dedicated herself to investigating methods of designing inclusive online courses.

Dr. Basdogan's current research focus encompasses a wide array of topics, including instructional design, technology-enhanced teaching and learning design, philosophy of technology, critical AI literacy, digital pedagogy, and digital ethics.